A GRAND *Calling*

Biblical Reflections for Grandparents

Robert M. Solomon

A Grand Calling: Biblical Reflections for Grandparents
© 2021 by Robert M. Solomon
Published by Discovery House Publishing Singapore Pte. Ltd.
All rights reserved.

Discovery House Publishing™ is affiliated with Our Daily Bread
Ministries Asia Ltd.

Requests for permission to quote from this book should be directed to:

Permissions Department
Our Daily Bread Publishing,
P. O. Box 3566,
Grand Rapids, MI 49501, USA

or contact us by email at permissionsdept@odb.org.

All Scripture quotations, unless otherwise indicated, are taken from
the *Holy Bible, New International Version*® Anglicized, NIV®. Copyright
©1979, 1984, 2011 by Biblica, Inc.™ Used by permission.
All rights reserved worldwide.

All websites listed are accurate at the time of publication, but may
change in the future or cease to exist. The listing of the website
references does not imply our endorsement of the site's entire contents.

Cover design by Mary Tham
Interior design by Lidya Jap

ISBN: 978-981-49-9123-0

To

My grandmother Gnanamah

("Wise Woman" in Tamil)

And

grandchildren Ella, Rebekah,

Lukas, and Benjamin

Contents

Part 2: The Practical Aspects of Grandparenting

Preface

As the number of seniors in our churches is growing, it is important to meet their needs and guide them on in the Christian journey. As a small contribution, I wrote *Growing Old Gracefully* in 2019.

Following that, some people suggested that I write another book for grandparents. In particular, I wish to thank Richard Tan, Christopher Tan, and Rev. Dr. Danny Goh for making this suggestion. This book is the result of their request.

The book is divided into two sections. The first section is an examination of biblical grandparents and their grandchildren—there are lessons for us all. The second section deals with various practical matters that grandparents often think about or struggle with. I've kept the chapters short to make for easier reading and reflection. I've also included a prayer at the end of each chapter to help readers turn to God—without whose help and favour we cannot carry out our responsibilities—as well as some questions to facilitate deeper reflection and practical application.

I have written this as a grandparent who is still learning and in need of improving his grandparenting ministry. This book is for my fellow grandparents, whom I hope will draw inspiration and instruction from God's Word, and strength from the Lord himself. May we encourage and be encouraged by our fellow grandparents in church as we think, pray, and care for our grandchildren. May we know "how to live in order to please God", and to do this "more and more" (1 Thessalonians 4:1).

To God be the glory!
Robert M. Solomon

Part 1

Grandparenting in the Bible

1

Grandparenting Is a Calling

When one becomes a grandparent, it is often a great occasion. Grandparents-to-be begin to talk more frequently about the new arrival in the family. They fuss over the preparations, basking in the special privilege of not having the direct responsibility of parents while getting to enjoy the delights of receiving a new life into the family. To become a grandparent is to pass an important milestone in life. It is like putting on a new badge of honour that everyone appreciates and values.

In biblical times, too, it was considered a special blessing of divine favour to live long enough to see one's grandchildren. Psalm 128 speaks about the blessings God gives to those who fear the Lord: that person is blessed in the family and farm, in his personal walk, and in his place in the life of the community. Finally, the psalm concludes with a great benediction:

> May the LORD bless you from Zion;
> may you see the prosperity of Jerusalem
> all the days of your life.
> May you live to see your children's children—
> peace be on Israel. (PSALM 128:5–6)

Given that the average lifespan then is believed to have been about 40 to 50 years—relatively short due to the impact of war, pestilence, and famine—it's no wonder that it was considered an immense blessing to live to see your children's children!

Today, people live significantly longer lives. The average lifespan is around 80 years, long enough for people to see their grandchildren and even their great-grandchildren. Nevertheless, there is still a lot of excitement when it is time for an older couple to make the socially-significant transition to grandparenthood.

For Christians, reaching grandparenthood is more than a social event: it brings with it a significant measure of spiritual reality and responsibility. The Bible states this responsibility clearly:

> Only be careful, and watch yourselves closely so that you do not forget the things your eyes have seen or let them fade from your heart as long as you live. Teach them to your children *and to their children after them*. (Deuteronomy 4:9, emphasis added)

These instructions were given by God through Moses to the Israelites as they prepared to enter the promised land. They received directions from God that they should:

- Watch themselves closely—they were to walk with God faithfully.
- Remember all that they had seen of the deeds of God, and the lessons they had learnt.

- Teach these to their children.
- Teach the same to their grandchildren.

This passage clearly shows us that we are not to retire from our teaching role after we have raised our children. Instead, we are to continue teaching our grandchildren the truths about God that we ourselves have learnt.

Our responsibility to the generations after us is made clear elsewhere in Scripture. For instance, the prophet Joel brought a rather disturbing message of impending judgment on Israel through the violently cruel Chaldeans, who would devastate the land like an army of locusts. It would be an unforgettable experience of divine judgment, a call to deep repentance, and an amazing promise of divine grace and blessings. The people were urged to take the experience seriously and to tell it to their children and their descendants:

> Tell it to your children, and let your children tell it to their children, and their children to the next generation. (JOEL 1:3)

There are at least four generations mentioned here: the "locusts" generation; their children; their grandchildren; and their great-grandchildren. Each generation is to impart their knowledge and experience of God to the next, passing the memory of God down through the generations. We are called to parent our children with the aim that they, in turn, will be good and godly parents. And while this is going on, we must still teach our grandchildren.

The word "vocation" relates to the Latin word *voce* (voice). It tells us that we receive our vocation when we hear God's voice. That is how Moses and Paul received their vocation when God spoke to them and gave them "marching orders", so to speak.

At His baptism, the Lord Jesus heard the heavenly Father's words, "You are my Son, whom I love; with you I am well pleased" (Mark 1:11). These divine affirmations came from two Old Testament passages that speak about the promised Messiah (Psalm 2:7; Isaiah 42:1). In short, the Father was telling Jesus: "You are my Son. You are my Servant." The first affirmation had to do with identity, and the second with vocation.

When we turn to God in faith, the abundant life that we receive has to do with these two affirmations. We belong to God as His children—that is our eternal identity. We also receive our vocation—all that God wants us to be and do. The apostle Paul was clear about his identity and vocation, both of which stemmed from his deep relationship with "the God to whom I belong and whom I serve" (Acts 27:23).

These twin pillars of the abundant life guide us when we become grandparents as well. In order to be godly grandparents, we have to be clear about our identity. We need to watch ourselves closely (Deuteronomy 4:9) and remember whose we are. We need to continue to walk uprightly and in faith and faithfulness.

At the same time, we need to continue living out our vocation. In this season of our lives, our vocation includes our role and responsibilities as grandparents. As authors on family life Tim and Darcy Kimmel point out, when we have grandchildren, we get a significant second chance to influence another generation of children and make an eternal difference in their lives.[1]

One day, we must give an account of that which God has entrusted to us. We will not be held responsible for the results, but we will be asked to give an account of how seriously we have taken this vocation, and how faithfully we have carried it out.

Prayer

Lord of the ages, help me understand that Your heart reaches out not only to me and my generation, but also to those who will descend from me. You are our gracious God. Today, I stand in Your presence with my children and grandchildren in my heart. Help me to remember my identity in Christ, and help me to live out my vocation to be a godly and caring grandparent who will pass on my faith and knowledge of You to my grandchildren.

Reflection

1. What do you remember of your grandparents? What lasting impact, if any, did they leave in your life?

2. How did you feel when you found out that you would become a grandparent? How did you see your role?

3. In what sense is grandparenting a vocation—a specific responsibility God has given you? How would you describe this responsibility?

4. Take time to consecrate yourself as a child of God and follower of Christ. Then commit yourself as a grandparent and ask the Holy Spirit to help you to fulfil your sacred vocation.

[1] Tim and Darcy Kimmel, *Extreme Grandparenting: The Ride of Your Life* (Carol Stream, IL: Tyndale House Publishers, 2007), p. 6.

2

Lois and Timothy:

Your Influence as a Grandparent

Numerous scholarly studies have shown that grandparents can have an influence over the well-being of their grandchildren.[1] A study of French-Canadian records from the 17th and 18th centuries shows that having one's grandmother staying nearby had a significant positive effect on one's health: such people tended to live healthier lives as children and as adults.

We know the same from personal experience: many of us can remember the impact that our grandparents had in our own lives. I did not have the opportunity to

meet three of my grandparents—two were already dead
when I was born, and one was living overseas. But I
grew up knowing my maternal grandmother. We lived
in a small house in a village, and our kitchen was in
another small hut nearby. I remember waking up in the
early hours of the morning to keep my grandmother
company in the kitchen while she cooked breakfast
for the family. She would be busy cooking while I
dozed off at the table. The sight of my grandmother
cooking, and the fragrant smells of the food, provided
a homely and cosy atmosphere. More importantly,
every morning, before I went to my primary school, I
saw living evidence of sacrificial love and service in my
grandmother. It left a deep impression on me.

In the New Testament, we read of Timothy, a
young pastor and protégé of the apostle Paul. Paul wrote
two epistles to Timothy, addressing him as "my true
son in the faith" and "my dear son" (1 Timothy 1:2;
2 Timothy 1:2). Paul reminded Timothy of his spiritual
heritage: as a half Jew—his mother was a Jewess and
his father a Greek (Acts 16:1)—Timothy shared Paul's
Jewish heritage.

In addition, Timothy was blessed to have a godly grandmother, Lois, and mother, Eunice. Both women were converted to the Christian faith—probably through Paul's ministry during his first missionary journey—along with Timothy. Theirs was a heritage of "sincere faith" (2 Timothy 1:5), for before they became Christians, these women were devout in the practice of their Jewish faith.

Later in 2 Timothy, Paul also remarks how Timothy has a godly heritage, being no stranger to God's Word. From infancy, Timothy was nurtured in the Jewish faith and was taught the Scriptures (3:15). This was most likely done by his mother and grandmother. We can imagine Lois and Eunice spending time reading the Scriptures to Timothy and telling him about God and the stories of His people. They must have taught him Jewish hymns and psalms, and initiated him into Jewish practices. Their hearts must have been ready when the gospel was preached to them, for their Jewish faith had already ploughed the ground for the seed of the gospel to be sown. In well-prepared anticipation of Him, they would have easily recognised Jesus as the promised Messiah.

After they became Christians, Lois and Eunice must have continued to encourage and nurture young Timothy. The totality of their faith in God and their new-found faith in Christ would have been an inspiration to the young man. This is the wonderful heritage that Paul reminds Timothy about.

This one dear grandmother left a lasting impression on her grandson, who eventually became a leader in the New Testament church. We do not have much information on Lois, but what little we know speaks volumes about her and her relationship with God and her grandson.

First, we can see that she loved God and His Word. She taught the Scriptures to her daughter Eunice, and also to Timothy her grandson (2 Timothy 3:15). Timothy may have heard his grandmother reading the Scriptures aloud from the time he was an infant. Perhaps he learnt to read them with her, and, in his teenage years, engaged in discussions about what they had read. Such a heritage is lasting and has a strong effect.

Second, Lois had a sincere faith in Christ (1:5). The Greek word translated as "sincere" means unfeigned or undisguised. Such faith is neither hidden nor hypocritical. When grandparents keep their faith to themselves, not sharing it openly with their offspring, their grandchildren will know little of their faith. When grandparents do not let their practice match their profession of faith, their grandchildren will not accept their faith, because they will see that their faith is not practised, and thus believe that it is not practical.

Lois, in contrast, shared her faith openly with Eunice and Timothy. She also lived out her faith with integrity. It became an infectious and convincing faith that was effectively passed down the generations.

What a rich heritage Lois contributed to her grandson's life! We can be challenged by her example and consider the following:

- Love God and His Word, and be seen doing so in front of your grandchildren—talk about Bible verses and passages you read, and read Scripture with them.
- Live out your faith sincerely, and let them see your love for God and His righteousness.

- Let them observe you in prayer as you handle life's difficulties with godly character.
- Encourage your grandchildren to love and trust God, and to read His Word.

Timothy became a pastor and bishop in the New Testament church. He became Paul's fellow missionary and his representative in Corinth and Philippi when Paul was imprisoned. He was one of Paul's scribes and co-wrote some of Paul's epistles (2 Corinthians, Philippians, Colossians, 1 and 2 Thessalonians, and Philemon). He also ministered in several churches. According to tradition, he died as a martyr at the age of 80, upholding the truth of the Scriptures that he had first learnt from his grandmother.

In effect, Timothy became a "living letter" of his godly grandmother. His name means "Honouring God"—what an appropriate name!

We may not fully know how we can make an impact on our grandchildren, but we can make use of the opportunity we have to pass on to them godliness and our love for God and His Word.

Prayer

God, our heavenly Father, help me to realise that You want to bless my grandchildren through me. Help me to impress upon them Your greatness and love, and to lead them to You and Your Word. Help me to live in such a way that they can see Christ shining in and through me, without obstruction and pretence. May Your work in me flow into Your work in them.

Reflection

1. How have your grandparents left an indelible mark on you? If you did not meet your grandparents or cannot remember them, imagine what you may have learnt from them. *(Hint: you can get some clues from the good lessons you have learnt from your parents)*.

2. How can you demonstrate your love and respect for God's Word? What habits related to the reading of and meditation on God's Word can you pass on to your grandchildren?

3. How would you describe "sincere faith"? How would it appear to those around you, especially your grandchildren? How and why might grandparents hide their faith from their grandchildren? How might they become hypocritical with regards to their faith?

4. Make a list of actions that God may want you to take as a result of your reflections. Pray them into your relationship with your grandchildren.

---

[1] K. Hank, I. Buber, "Grandparents caring for their grandchildren. Findings from the 2004 survey of Health, Ageing, and retirement in Europe", *Journal of Family Issues*, 30 (1) (2009), pp. 53–73.

3

Enoch, Methuselah, and Noah:

Being Godly Grandparents

Before the great flood, people lived many, many years, as Genesis 5 shows us: Adam (930 years), Seth (912), Enosh (905), Kenan (910), Mahalel (895), Jared (962), Enoch (365), Methuselah (969), Lamech (777), and Noah (950; Genesis 9:29).

Some people have problems with these lifespans, and believe that there was a mistake in the recording of the years or a cultural misunderstanding that affected the way the figures were recorded. However, many Bible scholars accept their accuracy, and note that after the flood, lifespans plunged to figures that are more like those we have today. Did God reduce the lifespans to cut short the damage that human beings could do?

Instead of troubling ourselves with the mathematics, however, we can pay closer attention to the characteristics of some of the men mentioned in the genealogy.

The first is Enoch, whose lifespan is the shortest in the list. At first, we might think that his relatively shorter life suggests that he was not as righteous as the others. But there is clear evidence to the contrary. Enoch is described as a man who "walked faithfully with God" (Genesis 5:22, 24), which shows that he was a man who was obedient to God and who was close to Him.

Another significant thing about Enoch is that he did not die like the others. Instead, "he was no more, because God took him away" (v. 24). Enoch is one of the two people in the Bible who did not die (Hebrews 11:5). The other is the prophet Elijah, who is described as being taken away to heaven by chariots, such that his protégé Elisha "saw him no more" (2 Kings 2:12). The phrase used here is similar to that in Genesis 5:24, suggesting that Enoch could have been taken away in a similar manner. We can conclude that Enoch was a particularly righteous man who was especially loved by God.

Enoch had a son whom he named Methuselah. There are many ideas about the meaning of this name. One common explanation is that it combines two words: *metu* (meaning "their death") and *shelach* (meaning "to send something"). To some scholars, this is significant because God sent the great flood that destroyed the earth in the year that Methuselah died. You can work out the arithmetic: when the flood came, Methuselah was 969-years-old, and is believed to have died just before the flood.

Enoch may have also been a prophet who foretold the great disaster that would fall upon the earth, telling his son and others about the flood when he was around. Indeed, the book of Jude in the New Testament describes Enoch's ministry as prophetic:

> Enoch, the seventh from Adam, prophesied about them: "See, the Lord is coming with thousands upon thousands of his holy ones to

judge everyone, and to convict all of them of all
the ungodly acts they have committed in their
ungodliness, and of all the defiant words ungodly
sinners have spoken against him." These people
are grumblers and fault-finders; they follow their
own evil desires; they boast about themselves and
flatter others for their own advantage.

(Jude 1:14–16)

Whether or not Methuselah was also a godly
man like his father remains unconfirmed. But his
name would have certainly been a constant reminder
and warning of God's holiness and judgment to his
community.

Methuselah had a son named Lamech who also
spoke prophetically when his son Noah was born,
saying, "He will comfort us in the labour and painful
toil of our hands caused by the ground the Lord has
cursed" (Genesis 5:29). Lamech could already see that
Noah was destined by God to play a significant role in
human history.

Noah stands out in this line of God-fearing people.
He is described in glowing spiritual terms in Genesis

6:9: "Noah was a righteous man, blameless among the people of his time, and he walked faithfully with God." Centuries later, the prophet Ezekiel would single him out as one of three righteous men, the other two being Daniel and Job (Ezekiel 14:14). In Hebrews 11:7, Noah is remembered as one who had a "holy fear" of God.

The fact that Noah "found favour in the eyes of the Lord" (Genesis 6:8) is all the more significant when we remember that the whole earth was in a major rebellion against God:

> The Lord saw how great the wickedness of the human race had become on the earth, and that every inclination of the thoughts of the human heart was only evil all the time. The Lord regretted that he had made human beings on the earth, and his heart was deeply troubled. (vv. 5–6)

God decided to send a flood that would wipe out the human race. But, because of Noah's righteousness, He instructed him to build an ark that would save him, his family, and every kind of animal life.

It must have been a lonely experience for Noah in a world that carried on in its wickedness with no fear of God. It is likely that both the "silent sermon" of his shipbuilding activity that signalled God's impending judgment, and his actual preaching of righteousness (2 Peter 2:5), fell on deaf ears. People would have been puzzled by his strange actions. I imagine they would likely have also mocked and taunted him for his seeming foolishness. Noah would have needed deep steadfastness to remain faithful to God's instructions.

Assuming that Noah took some 50 to 70 years to build the ark, we can safely say that Noah's grandfather and father were alive when he set out to obey God by building the ark. We don't know how much Enoch, Methuselah, and Lamech contributed to Noah's faith in God, but from the little that Scripture reveals, it is reasonable to say that they left a considerable influence. Significantly, Noah's grandfather remained alive until the flood came (his father, Lamech, died five years before the flood). Perhaps God gave Methuselah an extraordinarily long lifespan so that he could encourage and urge Noah on in his obedience. What a legacy!

We, too, can think about how God may want to use us to walk alongside our grandchildren to encourage them. For as long as God keeps us alive, we have a continuing ministry to our children and grandchildren.

Prayer

Heavenly Father, I realise that You are keeping me alive for a purpose. Help me recognise that Your purpose includes passing on my faith in You to my grandchildren. Help me stand with them, urging them to love and serve You, and to be faithful to You, especially in a fallen world.

Reflection

1. What key insights can you gain from reading about Enoch, Methuselah, and Lamech? How do you think they managed to pass on their fear of and love for God to Noah? How can you apply it to your own life?

2. Methuselah's name may have been seen as a constant reminder of God's impending divine judgment. In what ways can your life remind others of various truths of God's character?

3. It is possible that God used Methuselah to encourage and urge his grandson Noah to obey God completely. What might he have said? If you had to give similar words of encouragement to your grandchildren, what would you say?

4. In the years that God has given you to live, how do you think He might want you to walk alongside your grandchildren to encourage them and to urge them to follow Christ? What specific actions can you take?

4

The God of Abraham, Isaac, and Jacob:

The God of Every Generation

Abraham has an important place in our understanding of how God has been at work to save the fallen human race. He is mentioned in the Bible 312 times.

We first meet him in Genesis 11:27, as one of the three sons of Terah. In a pivotal moment in human history, the living God spoke to Abraham and called him to leave his home and set out on a momentous journey to the land of Canaan, God's promised land (12:1–3).

God wished to be Abraham's God and the God of his descendants. He made a formal "everlasting covenant" with him (17:7), promising him the land and numerous descendants. Abraham was to be "both a receptacle for the divine blessing and a transmitter of that blessing,"[1] through whom God would bless all the peoples on earth.

Thus, God became specifically the God of Abraham. He gave Abraham and Sarah a son named Isaac, to whom He also appeared. He made the same Abrahamic covenant with Isaac, promising blessings, land, numerous descendants, and blessings to all nations through his offspring (26:2–6). In this way, God was confirming His promise to Abraham and revealing himself as the God of Abraham and Isaac.

But God was not finished yet. He further revealed himself to Abraham's grandson Jacob, one of the twins born to Isaac and Rebekah. Jacob started life as a deceitful and self-centred man. After he antagonised his brother and others, he fled from home, fearing for his life. He then married two sisters and became the father of 12 sons. As he returned home to the promised land to be reconciled with his brother, he encountered God in a strange and mysterious way. He had to wrestle with God, during which he held on to his opponent until he was blessed by Him. God gave Jacob a new name, Israel, and blessed him. The deceitful man who was running away from his problems was now walking with a limp—because God had touched his hip—into a new day (32:22–32).

God also renewed with Jacob the covenant that He had made with Abraham and Isaac, promising him all that He had promised his father and grandfather. He became known as the God of Abraham, Isaac, and Jacob, a special name that God's people held on to over the centuries.

When Moses asked for God's name, for example, God replied that it was "I AM" and further added:

> Say to the Israelites, "The LORD, the God of your fathers—***the God of Abraham, the God of Isaac and the God of Jacob***—has sent me to you." ***This is my name for ever***, the name you shall call me from generation to generation. (EXODUS 3:15, emphasis added)

At the height of his ministry, the prophet Elijah found himself in a contest on Mount Carmel with 850 false prophets who served idols. After their frenzied prayers and dancing failed to light up and consume their sacrifice on their altar, Elijah made another altar, drenched it with water, and prayed to God: "Lᴏʀᴅ, *the God of Abraham, Isaac and Israel*, let it be known today that you are God in Israel and that I am your servant and have done all these things at your command" (1 Kings 18:36, emphasis added). Immediately, God's fire fell on the altar and burnt up the sacrifice.

When Jesus was challenged by the Sadducees who did not believe in the resurrection, He replied: "But about the resurrection of the dead—have you not read what God said to you, *'I am the God of Abraham, the God of Isaac, and the God of Jacob'*? He is not the God of the dead but of the living" (Matthew 22:31–32, emphasis added).

Peter, when speaking to the people gathered at the temple, also referred to God using His special patriarchal name (Acts 3:13), as did Stephen the martyr before he died (Acts 7:32).

While much more can be said about this special name of God, we can note the following: the patriarchal name of God reveals that God was at work in the lives of three generations of patriarchs. Abraham lived for 175 years; when he died, Isaac was 75 years old and Jacob was 15 (see Genesis 21:5; 25:7, 26). God loved each of them and wanted to bless them to be a blessing to the whole world.

There are a number of implications for us as grandparents:

- We must pray and do all we can to ensure that our God will also be acknowledged as the God of our children and our grandchildren.
- We must share God's interest in the generations that come after us.
- We are not just to receive God's blessing, but also to pass it on.

God is at work in your family, too. He wants to be your God, your children's God, and your grandchildren's God. Take and print a photograph that includes all three generations in your family. On the back, write: "Thanks be to the God of [your name and your spouse's name], the God of [the names of your children and their spouses], and the God of [your grandchildren's names]." Then let this photograph help you remember the spiritual heritage God longs to give your family as an inheritance!

Prayer

Heavenly Father, You took delight in being known as the God of Abraham, Isaac, and Jacob. How much You loved each of them and sought to bless them! You are the same God, who through Christ, seeks to bless my family, too. Help me and my spouse as we, the grandparents, seek to make You known and acknowledged by all the generations in my family. Be our God as You guide and guard us, and help us to be a blessing to others, as we seek not only to be recipients of Your love but also to be channels of it.

Reflection

1. Why do you think God renewed His covenant (with Abraham) with his son and grandson? What does this say about how He works in families and what His purposes are?

2. Study the covenants God made with Abraham, Isaac, and Jacob (Genesis 17:1–8; 26:3–6; 28:12–15). What did He promise them? How may Jacob have misunderstood God's blessings in restricting them to earthly needs (see Genesis 28:20–22)?

3. How were the promises that God made to Abraham fulfilled in Christ? Read Galatians 3:7–9. Why are all our spiritual blessings in Christ (Ephesians 1:3)?

4. How can you pass on these blessings to your children and grandchildren? List some specific attitudes, actions, and conversations that you can have with them.

---

[1] Victor P. Hamilton, *The Book of Genesis: Chapters 1–17*, The New International Commentary on the Old Testament (Grand Rapids: Eerdmans, 1990), 373.

5

Jacob Blessed His Grandsons:
The Power of Words

Mary grew up at the receiving end of constant jokes, stares, and teasing by schoolmates, neighbours, and anyone she met. Born in 1928 in the US with a cleft palate, she had a misshapen lip and nose, lopsided teeth, and could not speak properly.

Not surprisingly, Mary hated being born "different". As far as she was concerned, no one, apart from her own family members, loved her.

But then there was Mrs. Leonard, a teacher in Mary's class in second grade. Everyone adored her, but

Mary would soon discover something even greater in Mrs. Leonard.

Every year, teachers would give students a hearing test. Each student would take his or her turn to stand a distance away from the teacher and cover one ear. The teacher would then whisper something, which the student was to repeat.

This test worried Mary, who had a bad ear. She didn't want to give the other children yet another reason to be called "different"—so every year, she cheated on the test. She would pretend to cover her good ear, so that she could still hear the teacher's whisper.

Most of the time, the teacher would say something like, "The sky is blue," or "What colour are your shoes?" But that day, Mrs. Leonard said seven words that changed Mary's life forever. As Mary strained to hear her, she whispered: "I wish you were my little girl."[1]

As Mary herself recounted, God must surely have put these words into Mrs. Leonard's mouth. These seven simple but powerful words gave her a new sense of dignity and hope, assuring Mary that her teacher valued and loved her. This changed the way she looked at herself and others.

Words have the power to harm or bless. Words of blessing can change the course of our lives, as can be seen in the story of Joseph.

Joseph grew up in Egypt after his jealous brothers sold him off to some travelling merchants. He eventually became the equivalent of a prime minister under the Pharaoh of Egypt, where he married and had two sons. He eventually reconciled with his family when God led his father Jacob and his brothers and their families to Egypt.

After some years, Jacob sensed that he had not long to live. When Joseph visited him with his two sons, his father told him about how God had made a covenant with him (Genesis 48:1–4). Then, seeing his grandsons Ephraim and Manasseh, he "kissed them and embraced them" (v. 10). Verse 12 shows us that the two boys were sitting on Jacob's knees. Here is a picture of two small boys sitting on their grandfather's lap, probably gazing at the old man's face and looking at his large hands as he gently held their tiny hands.

This scene reminds us of how Jesus blessed the little children who were brought to Him: "And he took the children in his arms, placed his hands on them and blessed them" (Mark 10:16). Artists have depicted this scene by showing the children seated on Jesus' lap and being lovingly blessed by Him.

After Joseph removed his sons from his father's lap and presented them to him, Jacob placed his right hand on the younger Ephraim and his left hand on Manasseh (Genesis 48:13–14). This was the reverse of what Joseph had expected him to do; traditionally, the right hand symbolised greater favour, which would usually be given to the eldest son.

While placing his hands on his grandsons, Jacob blessed their father Joseph, saying:

> May the God before whom my fathers
> Abraham and Isaac walked faithfully,
> the God who has been my shepherd
> all my life to this day,
> the Angel who has delivered me from
> all harm
> —may he bless these boys.

May they be called by my name
and the names of my fathers Abraham
and Isaac,
and may they increase greatly
on the earth. (vv. 15–16)

Here, Jacob pointed to the God of his father and grandfather and declared that He was also his God. He then blessed the boys and passed on the Abrahamic covenant to Joseph and his two sons, further blessing his grandsons with a vision of numerous descendants: "In your name will Israel pronounce this blessing: 'May God make you like Ephraim and Manasseh'" (v. 20). The boys would become the forefathers of two of the tribes of Israel.

Here is a wonderful scene of a grandfather blessing his grandchildren. What a precious act this is, and what an inspiration for grandparents! Scripture tells us that our words can have a significant effect on others, as "the tongue has the power of life and death" (Proverbs 18:21). This is especially so with our children and grandchildren. Our words can make or break our children and grandchildren.

To ensure that our words become blessings and not curses, we have to check that what we say is constructive and not destructive. Constructive speech does not mean we avoid telling the truth or indulge in flattery all the time. God was angry with the false prophets in Israel who gave verbal messages by claiming all was well when it was not; their false speech had destructive effects on the souls of their listeners.

But there is a way of speaking the truth in love (Ephesians 4:15). Truth has to do with facing the facts and reality; it deals with *what* is said. Love, meanwhile, has to do with *how* and *why* it is said. In other words, we can convey difficult truths with gentleness, dignity, and empathy, in order to build people up in Christlikeness. Without learning how to do so, parents and grandparents can go to the extremes of spoiling their offspring or treating them harshly. We must thus watch what we say and how we say it, as "gracious words are a honeycomb, sweet to the soul and healing to the bones" (Proverbs 16:24).

Our words can also become superficial when they do not bring children into deeper experiences of God's truths and love. This happens when we avoid talking about God, or when our conversations remain trivial. Notice how Jacob spoke about God in his blessing and kept God central in what he said. We bless our grandchildren when we speak about God and what God wishes for them. When they grow up hearing such words of blessing, they stand a better chance of turning out to become men and women of faith.

Think about your grandchildren. How would you like to bless them? Or better still, how do you think God would like to bless them through you? When teaching His disciples about persecution, Jesus told His disciples: "At that time you will be given what to say, for it will not be you speaking, but the Spirit of your Father speaking through you" (Matthew 10:19–20). The same principle applies when we speak to our grandchildren: God will speak words of blessing through our lips. Just as He told the prophet Jeremiah, "I have put my words in your mouth" (Jeremiah 1:9), He will do the same for us as well.

Let us therefore seek opportunities to tenderly hold our grandchildren and bless them with the words that

God puts into our prayerful hearts. As Scripture says: "Do not withhold good from those to whom it is due, when it is in your power to act" (Proverbs 3:27).

Prayer

Heavenly Father, You have blessed me through many others, including my parents and forebears. Help me now to make use of my conversations with my children and grandchildren to bless them with Your life-giving words. May what I say remain with them as lifelong blessings from You, sustaining, strengthening, and building up their lives to be a blessing to others. May Your blessings pass on from me to my descendants.

Reflection

1. Think of some of the words and phrases (both positive and negative) from people significant to you that you still carry in your heart today. How have they affected your life? How do you manage the negative words?

2. How can we learn to speak the truth in love? What happens when we neglect either one of the qualities of truth or love?

3. How can we avoid having superficial conversations all the time? How can we build some depth into our conversations with our grandchildren?

4. Write down some blessings for your grandchildren. Seek God's help in finding the right words, reflect on them prayerfully, and use some of them for your grandchildren.

---

[1] Adapted from: John Trent, Ph.D., Vice President of Today's Family, *Men of Action*, Winter 1993, 5.

6

Naomi and Jesse:

Caring for Our Grandchildren

In the old days when tubs for bathing infants were uncommon, bathing a baby was a simple matter. I have seen women sit on the floor with their legs stretched out in front of them. They would place the baby on their legs and bathe the baby, pouring water, applying soap, and so on.

We can imagine such a scene taking place when we read about Naomi celebrating the joyful birth of her grandson, Obed, and taking care of him in Ruth 4:16–17:

Then Naomi took the child in her arms and cared for him. The women living there said, "Naomi has a son!"

Naomi's story was a chequered one. She was married to Elimelek, a man from the tribe of Judah, and they lived in Bethlehem. Unfortunately, there was a famine in the land, so they decided to move to neighbouring Moab. They brought their two sons along with them.

Elimelek died in Moab, and the two sons subsequently married Moabite women, one of whom was named Ruth. After 10 years, both of Naomi's sons died, too, and "Naomi was left without her two sons and her husband" (1:5).

In the meantime, the situation back in Israel had improved, and Naomi and her two daughters-in-law decided to go there. On the way, Naomi tried to persuade the young women to return to their mothers' homes, remarry, and find a future. One of them decided to do so, but Ruth clung to Naomi, saying, "Where you go I will go, and where you stay I will stay. Your people will be my people and your God my God" (v. 16).

Naomi returned to Bethlehem in a state of shame. Her husband and sons had died; during that time, this would be considered a curse and punishment from God. In fact, Naomi told the people to call her "Mara" because God had made her life "very bitter" (v. 20). She had gone away full, but returned empty. She seemed to have accepted what must have been people's secret judgment as she acknowledged that God had afflicted her and brought her misfortune (v. 21).

Naomi then found out that Ruth had gone to work in a field belonging to a man named Boaz, a close relative of hers. She got to work on getting Ruth and Boaz married, which they eventually did. Scripture reveals that it was the Lord who enabled Ruth to conceive (4:13). This was how Obed was born.

It was a time of great joy for all, especially Naomi. The women in the town noted how God had given her a grandson when she had lost all three men in her family. She now had someone who would renew her life and sustain her in her old age (vv. 14–15). They said, "Naomi has a son!" (v. 17). Naomi became a nurse for Obed; the Hebrew word *aman* means a foster parent, and is translated as "cared for him" in the New International Version of the Bible (NIV).

Thus, Naomi became the "foster mother" to Obed.[1] *John Gill's Exposition of the Entire Bible* notes that Naomi "became a nurse unto it, that is, after the mother had suckled and weaned it, then she took it from her, and brought it up."

The Bible stresses the important point that Obed was the grandfather of David, the great king of Israel (vv. 17, 22). In other words, Naomi brought up her grandson who would one day be David's grandfather.

What influence did Naomi have on Obed? What values did she impart to him? What habits did she inculcate in him? How did she encourage him, and what did she share about her faith in God? Would she have told him the stories of his ancestors and her own story? Naomi was a woman who had gone through difficult and disappointing times. As she cared for the boy and spoke to him, she must have had much to share and teach her grandson. And what he learnt from her would have passed on to his son Jesse and his son David as well.

Not much is known about Obed beyond the bare facts in Scripture. His name means "worshipper" or "servant", and he is listed as one of the ancestors of Jesus both by Matthew (1:5) and Luke (3:32). Perhaps, with God's help, Obed lived according to his name. His parents Boaz and Ruth were godly people, and his grandmother Naomi was a godly woman. With that kind of heritage, chances are that he lived a God-fearing life of a true worshipper of God.

What lesson can we learn from this story? It may be good to have parents carry out the primary parenting responsibilities of their children. However, in many modern families, where both parents may be working, a significant level of childcare may fall upon domestic helpers or grandparents. It is quite common for parents to drop their children off at their parents' home in the morning before they go to work, and pick the children up after work. We can often see grandparents bringing children to and from childcare centres and kindergartens.

Some grandparents may resent this arrangement, feeling that they have already done their fair share of caring for children and therefore deserve to enjoy a peaceful retirement. Some grandparents may be unjustly overtaxed to provide foster care. But most can share Naomi's spirit in participating actively and joyfully in caring for their grandchildren.

One secret is how Naomi recognised God in all the events and stages of her life. Even after she lost her husband and her sons, she could tell her daughters-in-law about God's kindness to her (Ruth 1:8). She talked about her God so much that Ruth wanted to make Naomi's God hers too (v. 16). And they all recognised that Obed's birth was a gift from God (4:13).

It is likely that a woman whose conversations were so full of God would have made an impact on those around her, including her grandson.

As grandparents, we can do the same. We can fill our hearts and lives with God and help shape the faith of our grandchildren. Who knows how our words and actions can manifest themselves in the lives of those who follow? God is at work, and it is thrilling to participate in what He is doing.

Prayer

Heavenly Father, I believe that all that has happened in my life was allowed by You for Your eternal purposes. I believe that setbacks can become stepping stones to a more blessed life. In my joyful moments as well as difficult periods, I am surrounded by Your grace. You have given me the joy of seeing my grandchildren and taking care of them in some way. Help me to use all my experiences to inspire them and to pass on my faith in You. You can see into the future, and You alone know what impact a spoken word or a loving deed can have on my grandchildren and their offspring. Thank You, Lord, for Your loving care.

Reflection

1. What do you normally share about to your grandchildren? What do your grandchildren know about your life? Do they know both the pleasant as well as the unpleasant aspects?

2. Reflect on how you are expected to care for your grandchildren. Is it a task that you resent or enjoy? Why is this so? Have you discussed this with your children?

3. What are some positive ways in which you care for your grandchildren? Are there areas in which you may need to give more prayerful attention?

4. What are your dreams for your grandchildren, their children, and their children's children? Turn your thoughts into prayer, asking for God's grace and power to dwell in your offspring.

---

[1] Pulpit Commentaries, Ruth 4:16; https://www.studylight.org/commentaries/eng/tpc/ruth-4.html.

7

Jesse and His Grandparents:

Passing on God's Grace and Graciousness

Jesse is not as well-known as other characters in the Bible. Compared to his illustrious son David, Jesse tends to stand in the shadows. But he should not be overlooked. There are so many seemingly unimportant characters in the Bible whose lives showed deep evidence of God's grace. Some of them are not even named—for instance, the unnamed courageous martyrs who demonstrated their loyalty to God in extreme ways and are mentioned in the book of Hebrews (11:35–38).

Jesse is mentioned 44 times in the Bible. In the book of Ruth, he is mentioned as the son of Obed and the grandson of Ruth and Boaz (4:17). He also appears in the genealogies of Jesus in the Gospels of Matthew and Luke. His son David became the great king of Israel, whose name was celebrated and connected closely with the Messiah.

His grandparents, Ruth and Boaz, are highlighted in much of the book of Ruth. It is a lovely story of romantic love, commitment, and family life (see Ruth 2:1–4:12). Ruth (a widow) and Boaz (the kind and godly relative of Ruth's mother-in-law, Naomi) fell in love, and he exercised his rights and responsibilities as a kinsman-redeemer to marry Ruth.

Ruth and Boaz are one of the most winsome couples in Scripture. We can imagine the impact they must have had on their son Obed, who was also cared for by the godly Naomi, as we saw in the previous chapter. They must have also had an effect on their grandson Jesse. What stories about God and His gracious and merciful ways did they tell him? What did Jesse learn from them?

Jesse became a farmer (like his grandfather) and kept sheep. Little is said about the relationship between Jesse and his son David, but Scripture gives us several clues.

At one point, when David was being hotly pursued by his irrational and paranoid father-in-law Saul, he sought an audience with the king of Moab and requested permission for his father and mother to stay in Moab with him for safety (1 Samuel 22:3–4). This indicates that David had a significant relationship with his parents, and that he genuinely cared for them.

David's mother, however, is unnamed in Scripture. According to Jewish tradition, her name was Nitzevet. There is some indication that she was a godly woman, for David—the songsmith of the nation—refers to her in one of his many psalms:

> Turn to me and have mercy on me;
>> show your strength on behalf of your servant;
> save me, because I serve you
>> just as my mother did. (PSALM 86:16)

It appears, therefore, that David was the product—at least in part—of the spiritual contributions of godly parents, grandparents, and great-grandparents.

In Scripture, at least in terms of the number of times and how he is mentioned, David towers above his immediate ancestors. Yet, his father Jesse is not forgotten and is given a special honour. The prophet Isaiah brings up the name of Jesse in relation to the promised Messiah: "A shoot will come up from the stump of Jesse; from his roots a Branch will bear fruit" (Isaiah 11:1).

In the previous chapter, Isaiah portrays the irreversible fall of Assyria, Israel's violent enemy (10:5–19). The prophetic metaphor is that of the felling of a cedar tree by God's own hand. People knew that cedar trees, once fallen, were unable to put out any new shoots. This is contrasted with an oak tree that represents the Davidic kingdom. Though it will fall into apparent oblivion, it will rise again; a new shoot will grow, demonstrating its indestructibility.

This shoot is the King-Messiah, whose character (11:2), rule (vv. 3–5), and universal blessing of peace

(vv. 6–11) is foretold by Isaiah. This is a clear reference to Jesus. The term "Root of Jesse" is mentioned by Paul in Romans 15:12, and in a similar form by John in Revelation 5:5; 22:16.

This has given rise to the concept of the "Jesse Tree". From medieval times, stained glass windows and tapestries have depicted a tree with Jesse at the roots and Jesus at the top branch. They provided a pictorial lesson about the history of salvation. Some parents and grandparents use a Jesse Tree to teach their children about Advent, the coming of Christ. Each day during the season of Advent, they place symbolic ornaments on the branches of the tree, accompanying them with a brief devotional that focuses on prophecies regarding Jesus, His ancestors, and the stories connected with them.

What an honour God has given to Jesse! It is not difficult to imagine that just as his grandparents, Ruth and Boaz, had nurtured his faith in God, Jesse, too, had passed on his experience of God's grace to his children.

What an inspiring thought for grandparents! We, too, have many opportunities to pass on God's grace and graciousness to our grandchildren. God will fully reveal how much we are able to bless them. The Lord Jesus spoke about how His followers will have God's life-giving grace flowing out of them to touch others: "Let anyone who is thirsty come to me and drink. Whoever believes in me, as Scripture has said, rivers of living water will flow from within them" (John 7:37–38). Though Jesus was specifically referring to the Holy Spirit (v. 39), we can note the principle here: as God lives in us with His truth, love, and power, we will be able to be channels of His blessing and influence. We have the potential to touch our children and grandchildren in ways beyond our imagination—all because of God's presence and grace in our families.

Prayer

Heavenly Father, help me to be a godly follower of Your Son, the Lord Jesus Christ. Help me to fear and love You, and as I do so, may Your life flow from within me to touch those around me, especially those in my family. May Your Spirit also flow into the lives of my grandchildren as I open my heart to them and let Jesus cross the bridge between our hearts. I commit myself to Your eternal purposes, and I pray that all that You have planned for my children and grandchildren, You will bring them to pass.

Reflection

1. What do you think David's parents' faith looked like? What evidence do you see in Scripture that suggests that they may have been people who had a godly influence on David?

2. Prayerfully think of what the future of your grandchildren and their offspring will be like. What do you think is God's plan for their lives? How can you pray for them?

3. How would you assess your relationship with your grandchildren? What influence are you having on them? Is there any area that can be improved upon or deepened?

4. What is the spirit (of the Christian life) that you would like to pass on to your grandchildren? Discuss this with your spouse and pray together.

8

——•••••——

Moses and His Grandson:

Busyness Can Affect Grandparenting

Many years ago, in 1986, Dr. Luis Palau was in Singapore to hold an evangelistic mission. He said something that I cannot forget: God has children—but no grandchildren. It means that no one becomes a part of God's family simply because his or her parents are Christians. Every generation must have a living faith in God themselves. It is thus important to pass our faith to the next generation.

One observation has been made about how faith is sometimes "inherited". The first generation who turns to Christ considers that faith as something to be *treasured,* as it brings joy to their hearts. The second generation considers that faith to be their *duty* to be performed. And the third generation considers the faith a *nuisance.*

This is quite a pessimistic view of how faith can degenerate down the generations if it is not passed on. We find this in Scripture, too. For example, we consider Moses to be a man of great faith in God. But then, when we come to the book of Judges (see chapters 17 and 18), we discover a Levite named Jonathan who became a private priest to an idolatrous man called Micah. And when the tribe of Dan took possession of Micah's idols, they made Jonathan *their* tribal priest, essentially making him the chief priest of a heresy. Jonathan was guilty of blatant disobedience to God, because Levites who were not the descendants of Aaron were not supposed to be priests (Numbers 3:10). And it was with his assistance that the tribe of Dan fell into apostasy.

This is a very sad story, because Jonathan was the "son of Gershom, the son of Moses" (Judges 18:30)— this heretical priest was a direct descendant of one of the greatest leaders of Israel! Unfortunately, this sad story is repeated again and again in many families, including our own today.

We can only speculate what may have happened in Moses' family. Moses, who served God diligently, had the inordinate task of leading the Israelites through the hostile desert to the promised land. At one point, he was so overwhelmed by his work that his observant father-in-law had to advise him to delegate some of his duties to others (Exodus 18:17–23). Nonetheless, he still had to deal with many complaints, murmurings, sheer disobedience, and rebellions. With all this on his plate, one can easily imagine Moses barely having enough time to attend to family matters.

His son Gershom, a leader of one of the Levitical groups, must also have been busy. The Levites had many duties connected with the tabernacle; they were responsible for the transportation of this portable temple and the maintenance of its furnishings. With the journey of the Israelites taking so many years, Gershom and his clan would have had constant work and plenty to do.

I wonder if the pessimistic view of faith degenerating over time, as described earlier, applied to this family. Was Moses' faith his treasure and joy, and Gershom's merely a matter of duty? Had the faith of his grandfather and father become more of a nuisance to Jonathan?

While Moses and Gershom die on the way, it is Jonathan who enters the promised land. Yet, it was during the time of the judges—and after Moses' and his successor Joshua's leadership—that Israel entered a time of national chaos. God had appointed these judges to restore order from time to time and turn the people back to Him; the philosophy of those times is summarised at the end of the Book of Judges: "In those days Israel had no king; everyone did as they saw fit" (21:25).

Jonathan fell into the spirit of the age, forgot his strong heritage, and brought disgrace to his grandfather's name. What went wrong? Who is to be blamed? Did Moses fail in nurturing his children and grandchildren? Christian biographies show similar stories in the families of some well-known servants of God; they were so busy in the Lord's work that their families suffered neglect.

One does not need to be a full-time pastor or Christian worker to see the same dynamics in the family—it can and does happen to many people. Busy careers, and even busy service in church as volunteers, can result in dangerous neglect with long-lasting effects.

But, perhaps, Moses was not to blame. When offspring fall out of the faith, godly parents and grandparents can feel extremely guilty and experience a deep sense of failure. At times, they may end up taking too much blame for things that may be beyond their control.

There are, after all, other factors that affect how a child or grandchild turns out. In the case of Jonathan, he had left his home in Bethlehem and was looking for a place to stay (Judges 17:9). Leaving his fellow Levites and their work to look for some kind of adventure, he had imbibed the spirit of the age, and his faith had eroded over time. This can happen in our day and age, too. In fact, it is a real problem among Christian families, as the ungodly and secular world makes major inroads into the mindset and lifestyles of the young.

As the Old Testament shows us, good kings can produce bad sons. Similarly, we are not entirely responsible for the way our children and grandchildren turn out.[1] So, what can we do?

As much as it depends on us, we need to make sure that we never become so busy that we neglect our families and the nurture of our offspring. We have to take time to effectively pass on our faith to the young, not just by teaching habits and rituals (which can be abandoned in a world of unbelief and disobedience), but also by demonstrating and explaining our faith. We can also pray fervently for the young, that they will treasure the faith as we do.

Prayer

God of the ages, I pray that the faith that You have put into my heart may continue in the hearts of my children and grandchildren. May the fire of my devotion and love for You burn brightly down the generations. Reveal to me if there is anything that I am neglecting in my nurture of the young, and show me how I can pass on the faith better and more deeply. Deliver my family from evil and the wiles of the evil one, that we may remain safe in Your loving hands and watchful care.

Reflection

1. What are some activities and commitments in your life that you can let go of to spend more time on and give attention to the nurture of the young in your family?

2. What is the place of Sunday school and children's ministry in church? What dangers are there when parents and grandparents farm out their nurturing responsibilities to the church?

3. What can be done to help parents and grandparents nurture their young at home?

4. What are some unhelpful and even dangerous influences in the lives of the young today? How would you help the young handle these various challenges?

---

[1] See Robert M. Solomon, *Raising the Next Generation: Meditations on Parenting* (Grand Rapids: Discovery House, 2019), chap 17 — "Family Scripts: Blessing or Bane?"

9

Jesus and His Grandparents:
Being a Quiet Influence

Jesus towers above all human beings, including His forebears and parents. When we examine His genealogy in Matthew and Luke, this becomes obvious. In his Gospel, the apostle John describes Jesus as the Word that was from the beginning, and the "one and only" (John 1:1, 14, 18). It is therefore no surprise that for many Christians, Jesus is a figure who stands apart from humanity as the unrivalled, unique person that He is. And this is true.

But we can go too far in this direction and forget the fact that Jesus had also become a human being and had grown up in a family, just like we did. He had earthly parents, brothers, and sisters, and He worked in His family workshop as a carpenter. He was at home for 30 years before He went out to engage in public ministry for about 3 years, before offering himself at the cross as an atonement for our sins.

We know who Jesus' earthly parents were—Joseph and Mary—and we have information about them in the Bible, though more about Mary than about Joseph. But what about His grandparents? There is no information about them except some references to His grandfathers in the genealogies.

Joseph's father is identified as both Jacob (Matthew 1:16) and Heli (Luke 3:23). Is this the same person with two names? Or could it be two different men, as popularly believed by many scholars? Luke's genealogy is believed by some to be that of Mary's family, as the two genealogies differ at various critical points—that is, Joseph was the son-in-law (the actual meaning of "son" in the text) of Heli, Mary's father.

According to a fourth-century explanation provided by Eusebius, a Christian historian, Jacob was Joseph's natural father, while Heli was his legal father (as explained by the Old Testament provision in Deuteronomy 25:5–6).

Who were Mary's parents? The Bible does not give any details. Christian tradition names them as Anne (or Anna) and Joachim. Some information about them can be found in the mid-second century text, *Protoevangelium of James*. Anne and Joachim were made saints in the Orthodox and Roman Catholic traditions, and St. Anne was the patron saint of miners in the area where church reformer, Martin Luther, lived.

Whatever the details of Jesus' actual grandparents, we can try to imagine how the relationship between Him and His grandparents would have been like. Jesus did not grow up in a vacuum, but in the small town of Nazareth among relatives.

There is a famous painting of Jesus as a boy, *Christ in the House of His Parents* (1849–50), by English painter John Everett Millais. It depicts a domestic scene with significant theological meaning: while helping Joseph with carpentry work, Jesus injures His hand. His mother Mary kisses Him to comfort Him while

His grandmother Anne attends to His injury. The point for our reflection is that the grandmother of Jesus is in the picture. The painting, of course, is the imagination of a painter who lived 1,800 years after the time of Jesus, and is based on Christian tradition.

There is another striking painting, *Holy Family with Grandparents Joachim and Anne* (1850), by Belgian painter Joseph Paelinck. Here, the child Jesus is depicted with His parents and grandparents.

No one can be sure how Jesus related with His grandparents. How long did they live? Did they have a role in His growing up years? Did they pray with Jesus? Did He ask them questions about their faith? We may never know the answers on this side of eternity. But it is not too difficult to imagine Jesus' grandparents taking time to read the Scriptures to their grandson and telling Him the stories of their people and God. Tradition has it that they were godly people who feared God, and they probably played a key role in Jesus' childhood.

What lessons are there for us as grandparents?

We may be called to play a significant but quiet role in the lives of our grandchildren. People usually

have little or no memory of their first few years of life.
If a child's grandparents move away or pass on during
the initial years of his childhood, they may not be well
remembered by the grandchild when he grows up. But
if their silent influences have made their mark, then
they would have had a significant contribution to the
child's faith and spiritual life.

It may be that God has called us to be a quiet
presence in the lives of our grandchildren. We may
remain in the background while their parents take an
active role in bringing them up. But it does not mean
that we must leave the scene. Rather, we can play a
supporting role and help the parents when they need
support and encouragement. We can make use of the
time we have with our grandchildren, teaching them
songs, telling them about our faith in God, sharing
stories in the Bible and of our lives. We can do all these
things with prayer and love.

We may be unsung heroes in the lives of our
grandchildren, but all that matters is the quiet impact
that we are able to have in their lives. This requires
humility, love, patience, and wisdom. We also need

to be good examples: how we walk with God can influence how our grandchildren walk with God in the future. We may not win any medals or honours for it, but God will be pleased and will remember.

Prayer

Loving and almighty Father, I thank You for the grandchildren You have blessed me with. Though I may not have a direct role in their daily upbringing, You have given me an opportunity to be a silent influence in their lives. Help me live in such a way that my faith is passed on to my offspring. Help them to see You in my life, and to see how real You are to us. Give me strength to leave behind a blessing, whatever my grandparenting role is or however it is appreciated and recognised.

Reflection

1. What is the significance of recognising that Jesus, the Son of God who came from heaven, also grew up as a child in a family surrounded by relatives? How does this help us see our responsibility to our loved ones as we seek to live a life that is pleasing to God?

2. Imagine how Jesus may have interacted with His grandparents. What might they have taught Him, and how might they have related with Him? What influence could they have had on Jesus?

3. Reflect on how you can be a "silent influence" on your grandchildren's lives. Make a list of how this can be done. What attitudes on your part would help?

4. What would you like your grandchildren to remember about you and your life? Are there any adjustments in your relationship with them that you may need to make? Take time to pray for your influence on them.

Part 2

The Practical Aspects of Grandparenting

10

Passing on
the Faith

In an article, author Erin Strybis, after both her grandfathers died in the space of 6 months, recalls the significant impact they had in her life. She writes: "What I remember most about my grandfathers isn't their interests or personality traits—it's their extraordinary witness to the gospel." She relates how, together with her grandmothers, they had invested their hearts and lives in their grandchildren. She adds: "And while it may not have seemed like their grandkids were paying attention, we were. In all they did and said, my grandfathers taught us about a life of faith."[1]

One of the most important commands God has given to us grandparents is to make sure to do all we possibly can in passing on our Christian faith to our grandchildren. Speaking to the Israelites before they entered the promised land, God gave a key command through Moses:

> These are the commands, decrees and laws the LORD your God directed me to teach you to observe in the land that you are crossing the Jordan to possess, so that you, your children *and their children after them* may fear the LORD your God as long as you live by keeping all his decrees and commands that I give you, and so that you may enjoy long life. (DEUTERONOMY 6:1–2, emphasis added)

This is an echo of an earlier command by God to the Israelites to be obedient and faithful to Him:

> Only be careful, and watch yourselves closely so that you do not forget the things your eyes have seen or let them fade from your heart as long as you live. Teach them to your children *and*

to their children after them. (DEUTERONOMY 4:9,
emphasis added)

A couple testified how that one little word,
"and", changed their understanding of their lives
as grandparents.[2] It appears in the two verses above
and reveals God's command to grandparents: they
are to teach not only their children, *but also* their
grandchildren. This revelation transformed the couple's
lives, as they embraced the responsibility given to them.

In fact, this generational approach takes an even
longer view when we read Psalm 78:5–7:

> He decreed statutes for Jacob
>   and established the law in Israel,
> which he commanded our ancestors
>   to teach their children,
> so that the next generation would know them,
>   even the children yet to be born,
>   and they in turn would tell their children.
> Then they would put their trust in God
>   and would not forget his deeds
>   but would keep his commands.

There are at least four generations mentioned here. The first generation are the "ancestors"; the second generation, "their children"; the third generation, "the next generation"; and the fourth generation, "their children". God's concern extends to those yet to be born, and godly grandparents are called to share that divine concern and vision. We are to have a long-term view of our responsibilities and prayerfully hope that our future offspring will be grounded in God's love and truth. Then we can be used by God to bless future generations.

What is the faith we must pass on? Christians use the term "faith" when describing our personal relationship with Christ. Such faith is described in the Bible in various ways:

> If you declare with your mouth, "Jesus is Lord," and believe in your heart that God raised him from the dead, you will be saved. (ROMANS 10:9)

> Faith comes from hearing the message, and the message is heard through the word about Christ. (ROMANS 10:17)

Now faith is confidence in what we hope for and
assurance about what we do not see.

(Hebrews 11:1)

Such faith must be passed on to our children and
grandchildren by encouraging them to have the same
faith that God blessed us with in His grace.

However, when the Bible refers to "the faith", it
points to something different. When Paul declared at
the end of his life, "I have kept the faith" (2 Timothy
4:7), he had in mind the "pattern of sound teaching"
and the "good deposit" that was entrusted to him
and that he, in turn, had entrusted to others, like his
spiritual son Timothy (2 Timothy 1:13–14).

While passing on "our faith" has to do with
participating in the work of the Holy Spirit by
sharing God's Word with others so that they can be
saved, passing on "the faith" has to do with laying
the foundations of a living faith, the content of what
Christians are called to believe. This faith involves the
central truths about Christ, as Paul spells out to the
Corinthians:

> For what I received I passed on to you as of
> first importance: that Christ died for our sins
> according to the Scriptures, that he was buried,
> that he was raised on the third day according to
> the Scriptures. (1 CORINTHIANS 15:3–4)

It also involves what we can consider as canonical, or standards.[3] In this regard, we have:

- Canonical Scripture (the Old and New Testaments that have been passed on to us)
- Canonical creeds (which help crystallise the essential tenets of our Trinitarian faith, such as the Apostles' Creed and the Nicene Creed)
- Canonical liturgy (the right way of worship, an important concern in Scripture, a right understanding of baptism and Holy Communion, etc.)
- Canonical biographies (see Hebrews 11 on the faith of our spiritual forebears; this involves telling the stories of Christians throughout history who, through their testimonies, urge us to follow Christ as they followed Him; see also 1 Corinthians 11:1).

It follows that we must know well and deeply value the Christian faith if we are to effectively pass it on to our children and grandchildren. We shall examine this further in subsequent chapters.

Prayer

Dear Lord, I thank You for giving me the faith in Christ my Saviour and for redeeming my life. I pray that this faith may also be found in the hearts of my children and grandchildren. I also thank You for the faith that has been passed on to me—the faith that has been preserved over the centuries through the testimony of Your church. Help me to know this faith and to cherish it enough to intentionally take time to pass on what I know to the generations that follow me.

Reflection

1. What is the difference between "faith" (to believe and trust in Christ) and "the faith" (the contents of our faith, on which we grow as believers)? What can you do to pass on both aspects?

2. Get a copy of the Apostles' Creed and the Nicene Creed (either in a hymnal or online). Study the contents. How do you think you can explain and pass on the central tenets of our faith?

3. Why do you think God was concerned about the right way of worship (see Exodus 20:5; Isaiah 29:13; John 4:23–24; Hebrews 12:28–29)? How does our worship affect what we think of Him and how we relate to Him? What can you teach your grandchildren about the proper way of worshipping the living God?

4. Try to build your library with good books that tell the stories of Christians in history. A good resource is a series of readable Christian biographies published by YWAM Publishing, called "Hero Biographies". Familiarise yourself with these

biographies. How can you pass on these inspiring stories to your grandchildren (tell them the stories, give them such books as presents, etc.)?

[1] Erin Strybis, "The Faith of My Grandfathers, Living Lutheran", https://www.livinglutheran.org/2018/06/the-faith-of-my-grandfathers/.
[2] See "The Incredible Importance of Grandparenting", https://www.familylife.com/articles/topics/life-issues/relationships/grandparenting/the-incredible-importance-of-grandparenting/
[3] See William J. Abraham, *Canon and Criterion in Christian Theology* (Oxford: Oxford University Press, 2002) and *Canonical Theism: A Proposal for Theology and the Church*, eds, William J. Abraham, Jason E. Vickers, and Natalie B. Van Kirk (Grand Rapids: Eerdmans, 2008).

11

Tell Them about God and His Ways

Our relationship with God is the most important one in life. We have a responsibility as grandparents to introduce Him to our grandchildren in a way that will help them to receive the truth about God and His ways.

One of the big worries that godly grandparents have for their grandchildren is the sort of world in which they live. As we read and watch the news and observe popular cultural trends, we may feel alarmed by how much the world has changed. The speed of life, the dependence on increasingly complex electronic gadgets, the coarsening of culture, the decline of social mores, the threat of war and violence, and the rise of sinfulness and evil can all add to our worries about how all this will impact our grandchildren's lives.

While we have little or no power to reverse trends or prevent the decline in faith and moral character in modern societies, we can still do something to help our grandchildren prepare themselves to live in an increasingly confused and confusing world.

First, we can *pray* for our grandchildren. We shall look at this in chapter 22 (see page 207).

Second, we can *teach and train* them.

Psalm 48, a song written by the sons of Korah, speaks about Zion, "the city of our God" (v. 1). Zion's beauty and loftiness is a matter for joyful singing (v. 2), and this is because "God is in her citadels"; in fact, He himself is her fortress (v. 3). Thus she is eternally secure in the Lord (v. 8).

Within her temple, we are led to meditate on God's unfailing love (v. 9). Then come some specific instructions:

Walk about Zion, go round her,

    count her towers,

  consider well her ramparts,

    view her citadels,

  that you may tell of them

    to the next generation. (vv. 12–13)

We are challenged to inspect Zion, its foundations, and its defences. The purpose is to be able to tell what we discover to the next generation and beyond.

What does this mean for grandparents today?

First, we need to understand the Christian faith as much as possible. This does not necessarily mean that we must go to a seminary to study Christian theology and history, though that would help if we can afford the time and money. What it calls for is to read and study the Bible—and to take time to do this in depth. You can get hold of books that provide good introductions to the doctrines and history of the Christian faith, or find many useful resources on the Internet.

Studying and gaining knowledge without also growing in our walk with God, however, can lead to knowledge that lacks depth and substance. It is important to seek to grow in our faith even as we seek to gain knowledge.

All this will help us lay the foundations of our Christian faith for our grandchildren. However, we do not normally have to do this single-handedly. Our grandchildren may be attending Sunday school and may be getting valuable input from their parents. In such situations, what we can do is to fill in the gaps and complement what our grandchildren are receiving. There may also be other situations in which our contribution has to be more substantial, such as when grandchildren may not be attending church and their parents may have lapsed in their faith.

Second, besides helping to lay the foundations of our faith, we will have to consider the fortifications and defences. This is all the more important today because of the way the world is going and its strong influences on the young, who will be increasingly exposed to false worldviews (for example, evolutionism and materialism), shaky moral foundations (human rights without reference to God or with anti-faith views), unacceptable habits (experimenting with sinful lifestyles and choices), and so on.

What can we do about this? We can protect ourselves and our children against these dangerous and debilitating "infectious diseases". We can "vaccinate" or "inoculate" our grandchildren by introducing to them the foundations of our faith, and telling them the threats that they can expect to face.

In Christian parlance, we use the term "apologetics" to refer to the body of knowledge that defends the faith and helps explain it to its detractors. The word comes from 1 Peter 3:15, where Peter calls on us to revere Christ as Lord in our hearts and to always be ready to "give an answer" (or in Greek, *apologia*) when asked for the reason for our hope. We can equip ourselves to do this by studying the Bible and reading good books on apologetics, such as C. S. Lewis's *Mere Christianity*, John Stott's *Basic Christianity*, G. K. Chesterton's *Orthodoxy*, and books by Josh McDowell and Lee Strobel.[1]

Some questions that grandchildren today may ask include:

- How can I know there is a God?
- Why is Jesus the only way to heaven?
- How can I trust that the Bible is true or relevant today?
- Why should I bother with church?
- What is wrong in supporting . . . (popular movements, issues, and alternative lifestyles)?

What happens when these questions are not addressed properly, or at all? Psalm 78 speaks about our responsibility to teach the following generations, as well as about what can go wrong if we shirk our task. The Israelites (who belonged to the exodus generation) are described in some sad sketches:

- They forgot what God had miraculously done (v. 11).
- They continued to sin against God (v. 17).
- They did not believe in God or trust in His deliverance (v. 22).

To prevent such a situation, God reminds parents and grandparents to tell their offspring the truths about Him and His ways:

I will open my mouth with a parable. (v. 2)

We will tell the next generation . . . so that the next generation would know them . . . and they in turn would tell their children. (vv. 4, 6)

Then they would put their trust in God and would not forget his deeds but would keep his commands. (v. 7)

It is clear that there is a lot of important work that we grandparents need to do, with a prayer in our hearts and enabling grace from God.

Prayer

*Holy and heavenly Father, You have blessed
me with the great deposit of faith that has been
passed down from the time of the apostles to my
present generation. Help me walk with You as I
review the central tenets of biblical faith. Enable
me to understand the foundations, and train me
to help answer questions and objections that my
grandchildren have in their minds and hearts. Help
me to seek not to win arguments for their own sake,
but to win my grandchildren for Your glory.*

Reflection

1. What does it mean to walk around Zion (Psalm 48:12)? What are the boundaries of the Christian faith? What are the lines that differentiate what is Christian and what is not—in terms of doctrine, ethics, lifestyles, habits, and opinions? Why is knowing such lines important?

2. Make a list of non-negotiable truths and practices that are part of the foundations of the Christian faith. Get hold of Paul Little's *Know What You Believe*, which deals with 10 non-negotiable truths of Christianity.[2] Read it and review your list.

3. Try to get hold of some of the books on apologetics mentioned in this chapter. You may also want to read or re-read *Know Why You Believe*, which deals with 12 common intellectual challenges to the Christian faith.[3] Make notes to help you remember what you read.

4. Reflect on the changes in the world and what kind of world your grandchildren might be living in.

What challenges are they likely to face as Christians? How can you further prepare them and "inoculate" them? Spend time praying for them.

[1] C. S. Lewis, *Mere Christianity* (London: Harper Collins, 2012, original 1952); John Stott, *Basic Christianity* (Downers Grove: IVP Books, 2012, original 1958); G. K. Chesterton, *Orthodoxy* (Chicago: Moody Publishers, 2009, original 1908); Josh McDowell and Sean McDowell, *Evidence that Demands a Verdict* (Milton Keynes, UK: Authentic Media, 2017); Lee Strobel, *The Case for Christ* (Grand Rapids: Zondervan, 2016).
[2] Paul E. Little, *Know What You Believe* (Downers Grove: IVP Books, 2008).
[3] Paul E. Little, *Know Why You Believe* (Downers Grove: IVP Books, 2008).

12

Imitate Me as I Imitate Christ:
Exemplary Grandparents

A country clergyman, nailing up a trailing vine, observed a boy watching him for a long time with obvious interest. "Well, my young friend," he said with a smile, "are you trying to get a hint or two on gardening?" "No," replied the lad, "I'm just waiting to see what a minister says when he hammers his thumb."

Children do not only hear what we tell them, but, more importantly, they also watch us and tend to imitate us. Faith is not only taught by precept, but also caught by example. It is for this reason that the apostle

Paul encouraged the Corinthian Christians to "Follow my example, as I follow the example of Christ" (1 Corinthians 11:1).

As keen observers of their seniors, children and young people are adept at recognising hypocrisy. We cannot tell them to do as we say, but not to do as we do. Our lives must be convincing evidence of what we teach and say.

This is why in the instructions given to the Israelites to pass on their faith to their children, it is emphasised that they should keep God's commandments in their hearts before they can impress them on their children (Deuteronomy 6:6–7). Personal faith and faithful obedience are prerequisites for passing on the faith effectively. Only when we intentionally follow the example of Christ as His disciples can we urge our children and grandchildren to follow our example.

The Bible speaks about how we, our children, and our grandchildren can learn to fear the Lord and keep all His commandments (v. 2). This is how passing on the faith looks like.

Paul spent time mentoring his younger protégés, one of whom was Timothy. In his personal letters to him, Paul wrote: "You, however, know all about my teaching, my way of life, my purpose, faith, patience, love, endurance, persecutions, sufferings" (2 Timothy 3:10–11). Paul not only taught Timothy, but he also demonstrated the Christian life for Timothy to observe. We learn best by watching and emulating. Just as Paul's life was an open book before Timothy, our lives are to be open books for our grandchildren. Notice the words used by Paul:

TEACHING. This word refers to all that Paul had taught Timothy, formally and informally. These teachings, which had to do with the "truths of the faith", were described as "good" (1 Timothy 4:6). Paul also described them as "the pattern of sound teaching" and "the good deposit" (2 Timothy 1:13–14), the fruit of divine revelation as found in the Word of God. It is no wonder Paul instructed Timothy to "preach the Word . . . in season and out of season" (4:2).

The teaching we leave behind is an important part of our legacy. It involves a significant input of biblical teaching in other people's lives. We can do this by doing personal Bible study with them, mentoring them, encouraging them regularly, recommending books, and so on. In a way, grandparenting is a mentoring and discipling ministry:[1] our grandchildren will remember what we teach them through our words and exemplary living.

WAY OF LIFE. The Greek word *agoge* refers to how we lead our life. The way of life is the basic lifestyle chosen and demonstrated; it includes our relationships and how we handle money, temptation, crisis, success, failure, frustration, joys, victories, and others.

As we teach what it means to live out the doctrine of God, we need to also adorn it with our lives of faithfulness, obedience, and love. The way we live has to match what we say, so that "in every way [we] will make the teaching about God our Saviour attractive" (Titus 2:10). Otherwise, we will lose the respect of our students and grandchildren. This does not mean leading a lifestyle of mere performance—young people are able to tell when we are being genuine or not. Rather, for our lives to match our teaching, we have to ensure that all our lessons are a result of personal transformation. And this can happen only if our lives

are rooted in Christ the way, the truth, and the life
(John 14:6).

PURPOSE. Purpose represents our directions
and motivations. It reveals whether or not we are
determined to align our will to God's good, pleasing,
and perfect will, and whether we really believe in it
(Romans 12:2). Our purpose will reveal whether we
are on a real spiritual journey. It will show whether we
regularly check our spiritual compass to determine our
direction in life, or whether we are just clock-watchers.

The clock represents our commitments,
appointments, schedules, goals, and activities—things
that drive our behaviour and condition our responses.
The compass, on the other hand, represents our vision,
values, principles, mission, direction, and destiny—
what we feel is important, and what we believe should
lead our lives.

Perhaps we are living our lives by the compass, but
our bearings are off. We are arriving at destinations we
do not expect or desire. That means our compass needs
re-calibration. Those dealing with ships tell us that
over time, the hull of a ship can build up magnetism

that interferes with the ship's compass. In such a situation, north, as indicated by the affected compass, is not really true north. To remove this interference, a ship has to pass over special coils on the ocean floor. Similarly, our internal compass—our central beliefs, core values, worldview, and motives—must be periodically "demagnetised" to enable us to continue our journey with accurate bearings. The coils, in this analogy, are the Bible, God's Word to us.

Are we living in a way where others can recognise the purpose of our lives? What evidence can they see? How can we, with purpose of heart, cling to God (Acts 11:23, KJV)?

FAITH. Faith is a relationship with the unseen God. How much are we plugged into the unseen reality of God? Note the definition of faith in Hebrews 11:1: "Now faith is confidence in what we hope for and assurance about what we do not see."

The life of faith is characterised by Paul in 2 Corinthians 4:16–18:

> Therefore we do not lose heart. Though
> outwardly we are wasting away, yet inwardly

we are being renewed day by day. For our light and momentary troubles are achieving for us an eternal glory that far outweighs them all. So we fix our eyes not on what is seen, but on what is unseen, since what is seen is temporary, but what is unseen is eternal.

A life of faith will show how much we live by what we hear (the invisible), more than what we see (mere pragmatism). It will be reflected in the quality of our prayer life. It will be shown in our peace and our uncommon reactions to life's uncertainties when compared with worldly ones. Faith also means faithfulness.

PATIENCE. Patience is a sign of maturity. It comes from a largeness of heart (in Greek, *makrothumia*). It gives space for human fallibility and foolishness. God himself is patient (2 Peter 3:9). Patience also arises from trusting God and waiting for His timing. The King James Version (KJV) translates it as "longsuffering".

LOVE. Paul's teaching reflected Christ's summary of the Law in Matthew 22:37–40 and His new commandment in John 13:34–35. Love, as described

by Paul in 1 Corinthians 13, is the fruit of the Holy
Spirit (Galatians 5:22). It is reflected in our attitudes,
words, and actions. It has to do with how we treat God
and others.

ENDURANCE. Endurance is running a spiritual
marathon. It means not giving up that which is
precious and important. Endurance comes from God's
power (Colossians 1:11) and enables us to last till the
end and to finish well. Note Paul's victorious statement,
"I have fought the good fight, I have finished the race, I
have kept the faith" (2 Timothy 4:7). Such steadfastness
is a gift of God's grace as we surrender ourselves to His
love and grace.

PERSECUTIONS AND SUFFERINGS. Paul
connected these to Antioch, Iconium, and Lystra,
where he suffered much during his first missionary
journey (Acts 13:13–14:25). How we live when we
are persecuted and when we suffer, makes the greatest
impression in others. It is the most convincing evidence
of a Spirit-filled life.

These are critical areas where what we teach and
how we demonstrate it will determine how well our

grandchildren will "catch" the faith. It is therefore important to examine how well we are doing in these areas.

Prayer

Heavenly Father, help me to fear and love You with all my heart, mind, soul, and strength. Help me demonstrate my love for You by the way I am eager to please You and do Your will. May my profession of faith and practice of it be consistent and congruent. May my life match my speech. Enable me by Your Holy Spirit to live in such a way that my life becomes an encouragement and inspiration to my children and grandchildren.

Reflection

1. Reflect on the power of example. What do you think your children and grandchildren observe in your life? What does it say about your Christian faith?

2. What does it mean to have our lives as an open book for our children and grandchildren? How can this be achieved?

3. Reflect on each of the eight areas mentioned in this chapter, and examine the lessons you are teaching your grandchildren on each of them.

4. Is there an area that needs greater attention? What do you need to do more of? Think of specific decisions and steps. Pray to the Lord about the Christian example you are setting—or failing to set—for your grandchildren.

---

[1] See Josh Mulvihill, *Biblical Grandparenting: Exploring God's Design for Disciple-Making and Passing Faith to Future Generations* (Grand Rapids: Bethany House, 2018).

13

Bearing Spiritual Fruit in the Wilderness:

Teaching to Swim like Salmon

Some people make a living looking for life in the most unlikely places. There are scientists, archaeologists, and speleologists (scientists who explore caves) who are experts in finding life forms in the harshest of environments on earth.

For instance, on the deep floor of the Atlantic Ocean, where there are permanent volcanic vents, where temperatures rise above 100 degrees Celsius, and where the noxious environment would kill any life form, there are species of plants and fish that have made their home. In caves in New Mexico, amid hard rocks and an acidic and water-free environment where biologists would not have expected to see any life, organisms have been found to be thriving. This is simply amazing!

Just as God has created such resilient biological life, He has also created equally resilient spiritual life. If we look carefully, the life that is found in Christ and sustained by the Holy Spirit can be found in the most unlikely of places.

We live in a world that is increasingly hostile to the Christian faith—not just persecuting Christians and the church, but also subverting the social environment in which we live. As Christians, we are called to live as light in darkness and salt in a putrefying world of sin (Matthew 5:13–16). But we are up against Satan, who continues to use persecution and temptation as the two major tricks in his diabolical bag, and who works in collusion with the sinful flesh within us and the sinful world around us. Only our redemption in Christ and the power of the Holy Spirit, whose sanctifying work is in us, enables us to live counter-culturally and to reflect the likeness of Christ in a mostly ugly world of fallen humans.

When we are Spirit-filled, we begin to bear the fruit of the Spirit: love, joy, peace, patience, kindness, goodness, faithfulness, gentleness, and self-control (Galatians 5:22–23). This (singular) fruit is but the very character of Christ. Its central quality is the love of God, which He has poured into our hearts by the Holy Spirit (Romans 5:5).

Godly love (*agape*) is connected with the other spiritual qualities. When love sings, we experience joy. When it rests, we find peace. When mature love waits, we learn patience. When it moves in action, we see kindness. When it deepens in integrity, we experience goodness. Furthermore, the loyalty of love is seen as faithfulness. The beauty of love is seen in gentleness, and its self-sacrificial nature is reflected in self-control and self-giving. A life filled with the Spirit will reflect Christlikeness, which is God's will for us Christians (Romans 8:29).

Yet, the reality is that we do not live in a vacuum or in a Christian holy huddle that is immune from the influences of the world. The dominant culture has negative effects on us, and provides many obstacles on the path to a fruit-bearing life. Theologian Philip Kenneson has pointed out how, in trying to cultivate each part of the fruit of the Spirit, we encounter obstacles from the dominant culture.[1]

- Love vs. culture of market-style exchanges (the promotion of self-interest and the commodification of everything).
- Joy vs. culture of manufactured desire (the pursuit of the wrong kind of happiness, the false notion that new is always better, and the rise of rampant consumerism).
- Peace vs. culture of fragmentation (the compartmentalisation of life, the growth of interest groups and factions, the excessive defence of "rights" and the idea that we need to be protected from one another, and the sanctioning of violence).
- Patience vs. culture of productivity (a mechanical view of time, glorifying productivity, and the speeding up of life).
- Kindness vs. culture of self-sufficiency (the promotion of self-sufficiency and autonomy, and

the failure to recognise our indebtedness to many
for simple things like our daily bread).

- Goodness vs. culture of self-help (over-optimistic
  view of human goodness and lack of attention to
  moral formation).

- Faithfulness vs. culture of impermanence (ephemeral
  changes and disposability).

- Gentleness vs. culture of aggression (the fostering of
  aggression, self-promotion, and the pursuit of power).

- Self-control vs. culture of addiction (the
  preoccupation with self and self-gratification).

This means, like salmon, Christians have to swim against the cultural currents to grow into Christlikeness. We have to be intentional in being counter-cultural and biblically-minded, and in developing habits of thinking and acting that enable us to withstand strong cultural pressures from the dominant culture.

It will be even more difficult for our grandchildren. The social environment will be more hostile against the cultivation of Christlikeness in their days. How can we help them?

It is important that we seek to understand the spiritual dynamics of the fruit-bearing life and Christlikeness. We must then examine ourselves to see how much of the character of Christ is evident in our lives. Some of the questions we can ask ourselves are:

- How do we bear the fruit of the Spirit?
- What is the connection between spiritual pruning (which can be painful) and being "more fruitful" (John 15:2)?
- What is the relationship between abiding or remaining in Christ and bearing "much fruit" (John 15:5), and "fruit that will last" (John 15:16)?

Christ must be revealed in us (Galatians 1:15–16). When our grandchildren can see Christ in us, they will be in a better place to come to Him and to cherish Him in their lives. Someone defined evangelism as opening our hearts and building a bridge to another heart on which Jesus in us can walk across. What a wonderful description of a grandparent's ministry to his or her grandchildren! This involves:

- Living a Spirit-filled life in total submission to Christ.

- Being close enough to our grandchildren for them to see us.

- Living transparently by opening our hearts and lives to them.

- Praying for the Lord who lives in us to touch the hearts and minds of our grandchildren.

- Encouraging them as they take steps towards Christ and as they bear the early fruit of the Spirit.

Who says grandparenting is boring? There is much we can do as we surrender to Christ and seek to do His will in our relationships with our grandchildren.

Prayer

Heavenly Father, You have chosen to live in me, together with Your Son and Your Spirit. Help me to cherish Your presence in my life and Your purpose for me—to become like Jesus, Your eternal Son. Help me to decrease so that He may increase in my heart and life. May I become a living exhibit of what You can do with a sinner like me, as You transform me with Your power and love. May I be Your letter to my grandchildren—Your message and Your display of Your splendour. May I take my grandparenting vocation seriously and let Jesus in me touch the hearts of my grandchildren deeply and permanently.

Reflection

1. Reflect on the hostility of the sinful and rebellious world against the gospel and godliness. How do you think this world will become more hostile against the Christian faith when your grandchildren become adults? How can you help prepare them for what they will be up against?

2. Go through the list of characteristics described as the fruit of the Spirit. Write down your own definition of each characteristic, and list how each could be expressed and lived out in actual life.

3. Prayerfully examine your own life and note where you reflect Christlikeness well and where you do not. What may God be saying to you about this?

4. Pray for your influence on your grandchildren. Let them see how you are faithfully following Christ, swimming against popular tides, and heading heavenwards.

---

[1] Philip D. Kenneson, *Life On the Vine: Cultivating the Fruit of the Spirit in Christian Community* (Downers Grove: InterVarsity Press, 1999).

14

Passing on
Good Values and Habits

On April 14, 1912, the Titanic crashed into an iceberg in the Atlantic Ocean, and several hours later, it sank. One woman in a lifeboat asked if she could go back to her room, and was given only 3 minutes to do so. She hurried down the corridors, which were already tilting dangerously, and through the gambling room that was piled ankle-deep in money. In her room, her treasures lay waiting to be taken. But instead, she snatched up three oranges and hurried back to the boat. One hour before, she would probably have chosen her diamonds over oranges, but in the face of death, her values shifted drastically.

Our values are principles and precepts that we hold dear. As we age, these can become more precious to us, or we may let them go because of confusion or doubt that arises when we are distracted and tempted by false, unreliable, or sinful values. If most of us are honest with ourselves and take a hard look at our values, living in a materialistic society, we tend to value material possessions, social recognition, and achievements. But there is a great need to value those things that are unseen, things that have to do with eternal and internal realities, and qualities and principles that bring us closer to God and to one another.

What are some of these values? We have already seen the nine-fold fruit of the Spirit that reflects the character of Christ. There are numerous lists provided by Christian and secular authors. One Christian website lists the following as top Christian values: faith in God, compassion and kindness, respect, patience, and loyalty. Another lists 10 Christian values that we can find in the Bible.[1] Let's briefly look at these.

WORSHIP ONLY GOD. We must make God the very centre of our lives and worship Him only. There are temptations to put so many other things in His place—things such as money (Matthew 6:24) or the luring glitter of this world. When Satan offered Jesus the splendour of the world, Jesus retorted by quoting Scripture: "Away from me, Satan! For it is written: 'Worship the Lord your God, and serve him only'" (4:10).

BE KIND TO ALL PEOPLE. Jesus summarised the Old Testament commandments in two statements: love God with your whole heart, soul, and mind; and love your neighbour as yourself (Matthew 22:37–40). Jesus taught some radical principles, such as doing to others what we would like them to do to us—the "golden rule" (7:12)—and loving our enemies and praying for them (5:44). These are difficult principles to live by, but they are key values for the Christian, and it is possible to live this way because of the power of the Holy Spirit who enables us.

BE HUMBLE. Jesus taught the importance of being humble, the opposite of arrogance and pride: "For those who exalt themselves will be humbled, and those who humble themselves will be exalted" (Matthew 23:12). He also demonstrated humility when He washed His disciples' feet, a lowly task reserved for the lowliest of servants (John 13:1–17). Humility was a key virtue of Jesus, as Paul pointed out in Philippians 2:5–11 when he urged us to have the same attitude as Jesus. The church fathers and other spiritual writers have emphasised that humility is the chief Christian virtue that opens the door to the others virtues.

BE HONEST. Honesty is commanded by both God's moral law (Exodus 20:16) and by Christ (Matthew 5:37). We are to speak the truth in love (Ephesians 4:15), a result of integrity in our hearts (Psalm 78:72; Proverbs 11:1, 3). Honesty will enable us to work diligently, be courageous, and avoid cheating others.

LIVE A MORAL LIFE. Jesus taught that we must be holy as our heavenly Father is holy (Matthew 5:48; 1 Peter 1:16). Our bodies are the temple of the Holy Spirit (1 Corinthians 6:19–20), and we must seek to live with purity of mind and heart.

BE GENEROUS WITH YOUR TIME AND MONEY. At the heart of generosity is gratitude, the habit of being thankful to God for His blessings. Our gratitude will lead to generosity. Jesus taught about the difference between having a good eye and a bad eye (Matthew 6:22–23). One brings light to the whole body, while the other leaves it in darkness. In that context, Jesus was talking about generosity, which has to do with inner health and holiness.

PRACTISE WHAT YOU PROFESS. Jesus spoke strongly against hypocrisy because of its deeply corrupting effects on the soul (Matthew 23:27–28). Hypocrisy is avoided by making regular confessions to God and repenting in His presence. Living as transparent a life as possible is good for us and for others around us.

DO NOT BE SELF-RIGHTEOUS AND JUDGMENTAL. Using unforgettable metaphorical language, Jesus warned against creating a big fuss over the speck of dust in someone else's eye while neglecting the plank in one's own eye (Matthew 7:3–5). Humility and honesty will help us to avoid this. We should not put down others to make ourselves look good, or rejoice at the misfortune and mistakes of others.

DO NOT RETALIATE. We must avoid angry revenge in the form of thoughts of fantasy or violent action. Jesus rejected these things and taught His disciples to learn to offer the other cheek when someone slaps them (Matthew 5:38–39).

FORGIVE OTHERS. God is merciful and has forgiven us even when we rebel against Him; we ought to reflect this godly virtue when others offend us. Jesus taught us to pray: "Forgive us our sins, as we have forgiven those who sin against us" (Matthew 6:12 NLT).

You might notice that most of the above values and virtues are derived from Jesus' Sermon on the Mount. It is good to be familiar with the teachings of Christ here, and to seek to live according to the principles He sets out for us. Jesus' sermon outlines the kind of people we ought to be and how we should relate to God, ourselves, and others.

Along with these values and virtues come good spiritual habits such as doing our quiet time regularly, punctuality, cleanliness, saying "thank you" and "please", helping at the dinner table, reading, listening, and sharing.

A grandparent who has thought through these things will be more effective in positively influencing his or her grandchildren.

Prayer

Heavenly Father, help me value that which is important, eternal, and good for my inner life. Help me to identify and understand the attitudes, words, and actions that please You. Help me to have the right values and habits. May my grandchildren learn from me and be inspired to adopt these values and habits as their own so that they, too, may live a life that is pleasing to You.

Reflection

1. Write down a list of your values. These could be in the form of short statements that represent key principles in your life. Take time to see if there are gaps (things that you have forgotten or not focused on). How would you like to practise these additional values?

2. Reflect on the 10 values mentioned in this chapter. Which of these can you strongly identify with, and which may need more attention?

3. Write down specific ways in which you can reflect these values and virtues. For example, how would you teach what generosity is, and how would you demonstrate it?

4. Make a list of good habits that you have developed over the years. Are there any bad habits, too? How would you impart the good habits and encourage your grandchildren to stick with them?

---

[1] https://www.christianbiblereference.org/faq_ChristianValues.htm.

15

Telling Stories with Moral Values

Everyone has heard about the ancient storyteller Aesop. Tradition has it that Aesop was a slave who lived in the sixth or seventh century B.C. He was a great storyteller, and his fables about animals have been used for centuries to teach children good values.

There are stories in the Bible that convey God's laws and principles. The Lord Jesus told many wonderful parables that not only conveyed valuable lessons, but were also so dynamic that even children could appreciate them. For instance, the story of the good Samaritan teaches how we ought to show compassion and mercy to those in need (Luke 10:25–37). The story of the Pharisee and the tax collector (Luke 18:9–14) emphasises the importance of humility and apologising to God and others for the wrongs we have done. The story of the talents (Matthew 25:14–30) illustrates the importance of carrying out our responsibilities with faithfulness.

There are also stories in Christian history that speak of Christian truths and values. For example, we can share stories of how Christians in the early church stood bravely and faithfully amid persecution, or how Martin Luther remained steadfast about what the Bible taught even though almost everyone was challenging him. Or of how missionaries left home, with no assurance they would return, to bring the gospel to distant lands. Or of the gripping conversion stories of people like Augustine, John Wesley, Charles Spurgeon, and others who were so instrumental in shaping the societies of their day.

Good resources for stories with moral values can be found in books edited by American author William J. Bennett. He served as the Education Secretary under

President Ronald Reagan and wrote a number of books to promote the teaching of good traditional values. His books include:

- *The Children's Book of Virtues* (1995), for ages 6–8. It contains stories and poetry with attractive artwork, and emphasises values such as courage, perseverance, responsibility, work, self-discipline, compassion, faith, honesty, loyalty, and friendship.
- *The Children's Book of Heroes* (1997), for ages 6–8. It highlights people, both real and fictional, who provide inspiration for children. While the book caters to American families, the stories may have a wider appeal.
- *The Book of Virtues for Boys and Girls* (2008), for ages 9–12. It contains a similar collection of moral stories and literature written by famous authors.
- *The Book of Virtues for Young People* (1997), for ages 12–17. Covering similar values as his other books, it highlights age-appropriate stories and literature.
- *The Book of Virtues* (1994), for young adults and adults; the stories can also be told to children. This was Bennett's original book; a bestseller, it is filled

with lots of stories, poems, and prose that highlight moral values and habits.[1]

There are also many resources on the Internet that we can use to find stories to tell our grandchildren. Here are a few that you can check out:

- "Christian Moral Short Stories for Kids" by Anna Spooner
- *Moral Stories for Kids* YouTube videos by T-Series Kids Hut
- Stories and other resources for children

A visit to the Christian bookstore will acquaint you with many other nicely-illustrated story books that have been written to promote the teaching of Christian values to children and grandchildren.

Children love to have an adult read books for them, though there is, of course, a time for them to also read the books aloud by themselves when they are able to. So, keep a basket of good books that you can pick from; if your grandchildren live with you, you may have more books that could fill a bookshelf or book rack.

Children love to re-read books and stories; they do not seem to get tired of repeating them. Perhaps it is the predictability of the stories that calms them down and lets them enjoy the stories. Do not hesitate to read books you have previously read. You can ask your grandchildren what they would like to read, and also introduce new books to them.

You can also give a treat to your grandchildren by taking them to the bookstore and library. Let them choose some of the books and get books that contain good soul-building stories.

Watching stories on television, tablets, and mobile phones may be helpful at times (there are numerous websites available), but reading a book is much better than simply letting children watch cartoon clips.

Sometimes, your grandchildren may test your storytelling skills by asking you to tell a story on the spot. So it helps to have a reserve list of stories. Even if you run out of stories, you can make up one on the spot. Like Aesop, you can use animals to create a story with a moral lesson.

You may have to adapt and improvise if you are telling a story. These days, dinosaurs are popular among young children; there are dinosaur books, cartoons, and toys. Your grandchildren may ask you to tell a dinosaur story (or whatever action figure or cartoon character they are into at the time). From time to time, my grandsons will ask me to tell them dinosaur stories. Now, dinosaurs are often depicted as mean and violent animals, so I will make it a point to tell them stories of good dinosaurs that are kind, compassionate, and honest. It does not really matter what animals feature in the stories; you can still use them to convey good values and habits.

More often than not, after you have told your grandchildren dinosaur stories, they will want to hear "one more story", and so it goes on. They expect you to be a limitless reservoir of stories. You can repeat similar stories and change a few details, or you can continue to exercise creativity by inventing new stories. Your grandchildren will love it.

There are other ways you can tell stories. You can use the material in newspapers and magazines that you are reading, if they are appropriate for your grandchildren. You can also help them reflect on what they read, see, and hear. A walk in the park can be an opportunity to "see" stories taking place before you: the little birds feeding together, the dog staying close to its owner, people throwing litter around while others use the rubbish bin, and so on. Just remember how Jesus used the birds and flowers to tell His wonderful moral stories (Matthew 6:25–34).

Learn how to be a good storyteller, and tell your grandchildren stories that will lay good foundations for their lives.

Prayer

Dear Lord Jesus, You were a wonderful storyteller. You told tales that stayed with Your listeners, stories that were enduring and brought people closer to God and to one another. Help me tell good, life-building stories to my grandchildren, who love stories and look to adults like me to tell them good and enjoyable stories. May the stories I tell them say something about Your love and trustworthiness, Your truth and character. May my stories reinforce good values and habits that they will not easily forget. By Your grace, help me do this because I love my grandchildren.

Reflection

1. Why do you think stories are powerful vehicles to convey truth and values? Recall some of the stories you heard in your childhood that have stood the test of time. In what way was your relationship with the storyteller, and how he or she told you the stories, significant?

2. Check out some of the resources mentioned in this chapter. Look for more such resources; take a trip to the library and Christian bookstore to look for resources.

3. Make a list of stories that you can tell your grandchildren, including Bible stories. If need be, practise telling the story. You can try recording it on your mobile phone to see how it goes.

4. Try to encourage your grandchildren to repeat the stories they have heard. Discuss with them, if possible, about what the stories teach us.

---

[1] All the books mentioned here were published by Simon & Shuster publishers.

16

Passing on Memories

ost of us can name our parents and grandparents, but it is often more difficult to go beyond that. Ancestors beyond our grandparents tend to remain hidden in the mists of time as social and family histories fade.

It is always moving to watch young people visit war memorials to look for the names of their forebears such as their great-grandfathers, grand-uncles, and so on, reverently touching their names on a wall that carries the names of heroes who perished in a war long ago. Memories of family members and their stories, when passed on to younger generations in family gatherings, can serve to strengthen one's identity and heritage.

Some readers of the Gospels of Matthew and Luke may wonder how the ancestral line of Jesus was so well-preserved when they did not have identity cards and birth certificates like we do today. Even with such documentation, we still have difficulty tracing our ancestral lines beyond three or four generations. So how did the family line of Jesus preserve the family history of Joseph and Mary, the earthly parents of Jesus?

It is highly likely that the names mentioned in the genealogies of Jesus (Matthew 1:1–17; Luke 3:23–38) were passed on from generation to generation. Such things were important for the Jews because of tribal identities. It was this identity that brought Joseph and Mary to Bethlehem, the town of David, when Augustus Caesar decreed that a census be taken. Joseph knew that he "belonged to the house and line of David" (Luke 2:4).

Each generation would have inherited the genealogical list of ancestors, and each generation would add its names to that list, so that the list kept growing. It is quite amazing that the list in Luke goes all the way back to Adam and God who created him.

Imagine domestic scenes in which grandparents tell their offspring the names of their ancestors. Curious children would want to know more about those people. Perhaps, the adults would be able to tell stories of some of their ancestors, stories that have been passed down the generations. In a multi-generational home, it is the seniors (the grandparents or great-grandparents) who usually have the best knowledge of forebears to tell these ancestral stories.

This could be one of the responsibilities of grandparents. They must pass on the stories they have heard from their parents and grandparents. If each generation passes on the stories, the history can go back quite a bit. Pastoral theologian Trevecca Okholm's book, *The Grandparenting Effect*, shows how cherishing and passing on family stories can enrich families over many generations.[1]

In Singapore and Malaysia, many families can trace their ancestry to other countries such as China, India, and Indonesia. My own father was born in India; he came to Singapore as a boy and settled here. I knew about my grandparents in India, and the name of a great-grandfather who was a Christian. Beyond that, the past has been forgotten. My mother was born in Singapore to parents who came from China. She was adopted by a Tamil couple and did not know the Chinese side of her past. But I know her Tamil mother, to whom this book is dedicated.

Passing on ancestral stories is not just a matter of giving information and names; there is more to it. Victor Hugo (1802–1885), the celebrated French novelist, witnessed distressing sights at the battlefield of Sedan in 1870, where the French were defeated by the Germans. Recalling the event, he wrote: "In the midst of the terrible plain I saw thee, O Thou Invisible One."[2] He not only mentioned the humiliating defeat of the French, but also testified that God was present.

This tells us that stories of ancestors can be told in the context of divine providence and presence. Even if you are not able to say much about your ancestors, you can say something about your parents and—if you are able to remember—your grandparents. It will be valuable for your grandchildren to listen to your story in the light of how God has worked powerfully in your life.

This can be done using old photographs and portraits, family heirlooms, and other objects from the past. It is a great experience to sit down with your grandchildren and go through old family albums and tell interesting stories about your schooldays, that memorable picnic, that time of hospitalisation, or that trophy for winning a race. You can tell stories about the other family members, your friends, teachers, and significant others in your growing up years, and relate how life was like in your younger days.

In telling these family stories, you can focus on the following. First, describe the events in a way that would be interesting. Second, portray the people in the story by describing who they are and how they had influenced you. Third, recall your own experiences and thoughts during the event—what you felt, feared, or enjoyed. Fourth, share what you learnt about God and how you may have felt His presence or favour, either during the event or perhaps upon later reflection.

Passing on stories orally can have a greater impact because it involves relationship and personal involvement. Children love hearing stories told to them, and can carry the contents and the lessons for life. If your stories have made an impact on the young, they may be passed on to younger generations, and some of the stories may become family treasures.

Besides telling stories from the past, grandparents can also help create fresh memories for their grandchildren. This can be done in many ways. Dr. Lynn Wilson, a professor of early childhood development and author of *A Handbook For Grandparents*, lists 700 activities that grandparents can use to create memories for their grandchildren.[3] Some examples include taking photos of your grandchildren at the same spot (such as a park) every year and building the collection; keeping a journal of "Memories of My Grandchild" (that will be read later with greater appreciation); and having a sleep over at your place for your grandchildren—with all their cousins.

Grandparents can be good storytellers and memory makers. It is sad when good and valuable memories die with the older generation without being passed on to the young. As grandparents, we have many experiences and stories to share. We are archivists and historians, like the ancient storytellers who regaled their listeners with interesting stories around a campfire at night— stories that will long be remembered and passed on for generations. Scholars use the term "oral tradition" or "oral history" to describe this process.

If you visit the National Archives of Singapore, you will find recordings of oral interviews with old Singaporeans who tell engaging stories of life in old Singapore—of colonial times, education, family, war, and troubled times as well as happy times. It was felt that a generation was dying with these treasures locked away and untold in their memories, and I am glad the historians found value in preserving them. I have listened to some of these old stories and found them to be of great interest.

How wonderful it would be if we grandparents find time and opportunity to tell our stories to our grandchildren!

Prayer

Almighty and loving Father, my life has been a journey, and You have been present throughout, both on good days and difficult ones. I have many stories to tell of Your goodness and faithfulness, and I pray that You will bring them to my memory so that I can give thanks to You and share them with my children and grandchildren. Help me to also use my creativity to help make new memories for my grandchildren—memories that will bring them to an awareness of Your love and truth, of Your presence and faithfulness.

Reflection

1. Meditate on Psalm 23. Consider the various places and experiences mentioned by the psalmist: the place where he realised God was his Shepherd, the still waters, the green pastures, the paths of righteousness, the valley of the shadow of death, protection from enemies, vindication, and the hope for eternal life in God's house. Use your meditation to write out your own story of different places, experiences, people, and the presence of God. You can share this story with your grandchildren.

2. In the congregational and family worship in ancient Israel, there was a lot of storytelling (Psalm 44, 78; Exodus 13:14–16). Reflect on the importance of such storytelling and how you can incorporate it into your family life and activities.

3. Make a list of ways in which you can create some good memories for your grandchildren. Plan to put these into action.

4. Discuss your experience of sharing memories with your offspring with other grandparents in church. Consider having a project where you can record your oral histories or have a special activity with the young ones, where one of the things you can do is to tell your interesting and unforgettable stories.

[1] Trevecca Okholm, *The Grandparenting Effect: Bridging Generations One Story at a Time* (Eugene, OR: Cascade Books, 2020).

[2] http://www.moreillustrations.com/Illustrations/history.html.

[3] Lynn Wilson, *A Handbook for Grandparents: Over 700 Creative Things to Do and Make With Your Grandchild* (Victoria, BC, Canada: Friesen Press, 2015).

17

Passing Wisdom vs. Giving Advice

Our own experiences and observations of fellow grandparents reveal that there are often tensions and conflicts between grandparents and parents regarding the care and upbringing of children. This may be heightened when our children and grandchildren live with us in the same household. One grandparent told me that while he could see why this arrangement had its conveniences (albeit more for his son's family), it also led to possible tension. Is not a man, he asked me, to leave his father and mother and cleave to his wife (Genesis 2:24)?

In a Mott Poll Report published in 2020 by C. S. Mott Children's Hospital in Michigan, US, a nationwide survey of 2,000 parents of children below the age of 18 produced some interesting findings:[1]

- 6 percent of parents reported major differences of opinion, while 37 percent reported minor disagreements.
- 15 percent said that disagreements had negative effects on the relationship between grandparents and their grandchildren.
- 40 percent observed that grandparents were too soft on their grandchildren, while 14 percent said they were too tough.

The most common areas of disagreement were discipline (57 percent), meals and snacks (44 percent), and television/screen time (36 percent). Other disagreements were about manners (27 percent), health and safety (25 percent), favouritism (22 percent), bedtime (21 percent), and sharing photos and information on social media (10 percent).

According to the survey, 43 percent of parents asked a grandparent to change their behaviour in line with the parent's choices or rules. Of these, 47 percent of grandparents changed their behaviour, 36 percent agreed to the request but did not change their behaviour, and 17 percent refused to change.

On average, 15 percent of parents limited the amount of time that their children got with their grandparents. This was more common when grandparents did not respect parenting choices: 32 percent of parents limited the contact time with grandparents who agreed to change their behaviour but did not, and 42 percent imposed limits when a grandparent refused to change. There is such a thing as toxic grandparenting![2]

The survey results reflect the multifaceted issues concerning the relationship and potential conflicts between grandparents and parents over grandchildren. Why are there such conflicts? There are some general reasons, though many others depend on the family situation.

To begin with, when there are two sets of parents in the home, the issue of "Who has more expertise?" often becomes a source of tension. Younger people (the parents) tend to rely more on what they read or see on the Internet and social media regarding the care of children and their development, while older people (the grandparents) tend to rely on experience and what they have learnt from their own seniors. Hence the potential conflict between Internet-gained knowledge and that gained from experience and traditional practice. When younger people consider the former as the primary source of parenting expertise, their parents may feel frustrated and resentful when their advice is ignored.

In this, it will help if there is give and take on both sides. Younger people may have to courteously and seriously take into account what their parents say—sometimes they are right! There are also biblical instructions that they need to reflect on carefully. The fourth commandment in God's moral law instructs children (including adult children) to honour their parents (Exodus 20:12), a divine principle that was reiterated by Jesus and the apostles (Matthew 15:4, 19:19; Ephesians 6:1–3).

When Jesus was 12, near the Jewish traditional age of becoming a man, He realised that His parents "did not understand" what He said and knew. Yet, He went home with them from Jerusalem and "was obedient to them" (Luke 2:50–51). He kept every commandment, including the fourth.

We might say that when Jesus was much older, the rules and relationships would have had to change. Yes, in His identity and ministry, He was totally committed to His heavenly Father and His will. But that did not preclude Him listening to His earthly mother's suggestion to do something about the wine when it ran out at a wedding at Cana (John 2:3–5).

But there were also instances when Jesus seemingly ignored His mother. In a crowded house, He was told that His mother and brothers were outside seeking to speak to Him. They had come because they had heard that Jesus was neglecting His meals; they thought He had gone mad, and wanted to "take charge of him" (Mark 3:21). But Jesus replied rather curtly that it was those who did God's will who were really His mother and brothers (vv. 33–35).

Throughout this time, however, Jesus never lost one bit of love and respect for His mother. At the cross, He specifically made sure that Mary was to be taken care of after His death (John 19:26–27). The New Testament also highlights the importance of respecting seniors and elders (1 Timothy 5:1–2, 17).

At the same time, grandparents might want to think through some of their own assumptions about themselves. While it might be true that grandparents often have more experience raising a family, it cannot be assumed that they are the authority and expert in every aspect. On their part, grandparents must also recognise that their children may be better informed than they are. The Internet has given parents today access to a breadth of information and new studies that were simply not available to us in the past. Hence, it is not always helpful to think, "This is the way we did it." Moreover, some issues that parents today have to deal with may also be new, such as the use and abuse of phones and social media. The reality of grandparenting as we know it is going through significant changes.[3]

It is necessary to recognise that your children are the parents of your grandchildren, not you. It is not right to take over and usurp the authority of the parents or their parenting goals and aspirations.

There is a difference between sharing our wisdom and giving unsolicited advice, especially when it brings us into serious contention with our children. In passages in the book of Proverbs on the wisdom of parents for their children, the tone is not one of coercion, but gentle persuasion (see Proverbs 9:1–6). We also note that "the teaching of the wise is a fountain of life" (13:14), and that "grey hair is a crown of splendour; it is attained in the way of righteousness" (16:31). This is followed by the words, "Better a patient person than a warrior, one with self-control than one who takes a city" (v. 32). Wisdom and patience go together.

In practice, when we are called upon to share our experience, we can readily do so, not so much to lecture our children, but to assist them in raising their children with respect, love, and gentleness. When we see things done wrongly, we can point it out to them. If they listen, that's good. If not, we can try to persuade them and leave the matter to them, without nagging or coercion. Unless we feel that child abuse is taking place, we should hold our peace, pray, and try to be supportive of our children's efforts in raising their children. There is, after all, a difference between intervention and interference.[4]

At the end of the day, our main aim is not to win arguments, but to win our children and grandchildren to the Lord's grace and love. We should be friends and partners to our children, not their bosses or employers. With the right perspective, we should minimise their stress and challenges.

Prayer

Heavenly Father, I thank You for the children You have given my spouse and me, and the grandchildren You have given us. We hold in sacred trust the generations after us, and we pray that You will fill us with Your grace and love, with humility and wisdom, to be able to lend support to our children in their parenting role. Help us to be an asset rather than a liability, a wise voice rather than nagging and irritating advisors. Help us to prayerfully share our wisdom, gently and patiently, for we know You are sovereign and watch over us all. We are in Your safe and loving hands, heavenly Father.

Reflection

••••

1. Review the Mott Poll Report and some of the issues highlighted that point to potential conflicts between grandparents and parents. Which of these resonate with your own experience?

2. Why is it not good for your grandchildren to witness your arguments with their parents, especially when it leads to loud arguments? What may they think and feel in such situations? How can you take the matter "offline" and away from your grandchildren?

3. Reflect on the differences in expectations, knowledge, and experience between grandparents and parents. What may be similar, especially from the biblical point of view? Are there presumptions and expectations on your part that would need further reflection and revision?

4. Consider the difference between sharing wisdom and giving advice, especially when it is unsolicited. How can you exercise wisdom, patience, and forgiveness when you have arguments with your children? Why

is giving in a part of this process? How can we give in and surrender the matter to God?

[1] Mott Poll Report, "When Parents and Grandparents Disagree", https://mottpoll.org/reports/when-parents-and-grandparents-disagree.

[2] "Toxic Grandparent Checklist: 10 Signs That There Is a Problem", https://toxicties.com/toxic-grandparent-signs/.

[3] See Laura Trapp, *Grandparenting in a Digital Age* (Lanham, MD: Rowman & Littlefield Publishing Group, 2018).

[4] For a list of eight situations when intervention is needed, see Jennifer Kelly Geddes, "These Are the 8 Times Grandparents Need to Intervene", https://www.considerable.com/life/family/when-should-grandparents-speak-up/. The eight situations are rudeness, developmental delays, safety, nutrition, physical or sexual abuse, true neglect, substance abuse by the parent or mental health issue, and imminent harm to the grandchild.

18

Grandparents and Parents Are Partners

It is a common saying that grandparents are guilty of sabotaging their children's efforts in bringing up their children. They are said to feed their grandchildren food that is forbidden by their parents— such as sugary and fried foods. They are also alleged to spoil them with lax discipline, or by giving them permission to break their parents' rules.

But this need not be so. Grandparents and parents are not competitors; rather, they are partners. This partnership creates a positive environment in which both generations know their roles and acknowledge each other's roles and responsibilities. In this regard, it must be recognised by grandparents that the primary, essential role of parenting belongs to the parents; grandparents have a secondary and supportive role of helping and encouraging their children to fulfil *their* parenting responsibilities.

The implication of this is that the final decisions regarding our grandchildren, their wellbeing, and their upbringing belong to their parents. We cannot usurp that role, unless the parents are neglectful or abusive. At the same time, we should not go to the other extreme and totally withdraw from the upbringing of our grandchildren. We must recognise that we do have a positive role to play.

Here is where the idea of partnership comes in. When grandparents recognise their supportive role and give as much encouragement as possible to their children in the raising of the grandchildren, there is potential for much good. This is especially appreciated in the case of grandchildren who suffer from medical conditions that require greater care and support. Parents of such children go through considerable stress making adjustments, and caring, wise, and loving grandparents can assist as supportive partners.

The Bible has many examples of positive partnerships. We can think of one between Paul and Barnabas. Barnabas, as indicated by his name meaning "son of encouragement", was a man who was essentially an encourager. After the apostle Paul was converted, he had to overcome the fear held among Christians that he was still a persecutor of the church and had not really changed (Acts 9:26). Many kept their distance. But Barnabas believed that Paul's conversion was genuine, and brought him to the apostles in Jerusalem, speaking for him. As a result, Paul gained the confidence of the apostles and the other believers.

Paul was sent home to Tarsus because of the commotion arising over him in Jerusalem, for he was a brilliant debater and apologist for the gospel. He spent many years there in relative oblivion, until Barnabas went to look for him following a revival in Antioch (11:25–26). The two men eventually became partners in mission (Acts 13–14). During their missionary journey, the descriptions of their partnership shifted

from "Barnabas and Paul" to "Paul and Barnabas".
Paul began to take prominence in the partnership, and
Barnabas was happy to play second fiddle.

As they prepared to embark on another missionary
journey, both men had a "sharp disagreement"
regarding the young John Mark who had accompanied
them on the earlier journey but had abandoned
them halfway. Paul did not want to take Mark along,
but Barnabas wanted to give him a second chance.
They disagreed so strongly that they split into two
missionary groups (15:36–40). Scripture does not say
what eventually happened to the partnership between
Paul and Barnabas; perhaps Barnabas realised that he
was no longer needed to mentor Paul and moved on to
mentor others.

On his part, Paul, in his old age and just before his
martyrdom, asked for Mark to visit him "because he
is helpful to me in my ministry" (2 Timothy 4:11). It
appears that Paul may have realised that his judgment
of Mark was hasty and that Barnabas was right; so
he reconciled with Mark and partnered with him
(Colossians 4:10).

We can apply these observations and insights to the relationship between grandparents and parents. Before we became grandparents, we were parents, and we have gathered experience along the way. When our children become parents, we naturally want to coach them in parenting, thinking that we can share our knowledge and experience. Initially, our children may be grateful and accept our help as they find their footing as young parents. Over time, however, as they gain experience and become more confident, they may want to exert their parenting role. We then find ourselves in a "second-fiddle" role in the upbringing of our grandchildren. It is a transition that we are challenged to graciously accept with grace and maturity.

We can end up in serious arguments with our children over parenting goals, strategies, and skills. Or, we can wisely try to find resolution and reconciliation by accepting our secondary and supportive role. Sometimes, we may be wrong in our opinions—but even if we are right, we have to remember that it is not about winning the argument. Rather, it is about the joy of knowing that God's will and mission is being accomplished in the lives of our loved ones. In times when we feel that our children are making mistakes, let us continue to hope prayerfully that they will be protected and will eventually succeed.

We can imagine the kind of partnership between Timothy's grandmother Lois and mother Eunice (2 Timothy 1:5; 3:14–15). They shared their faith in Christ, the important task of bringing up young Timothy in the faith, and the need to model the Christian life. Timothy's father was Greek; the Bible does not say if he was a believer. Eunice found spiritual support in her mother, and together, they were spiritual partners in bringing Timothy up in the faith.

Grandparents can leave a positive impact on their grandchildren when they demonstrate their love for the children's parents. This has a nurturing influence on the young when they see their parents and grandparents functioning as an amiable and loving team, and not as argumentative competitors.

Demonstrating this love in practical ways can include:

- Complimenting our children whenever possible.

- Praying together with our children for our grandchildren.
- Supporting our children in their parenting decisions in front of our grandchildren. (Arguments or differences should be kept away from the grandchildren). We should consider ways of honouring our grandchildren's father and mother.[1]
- Showing physical affection for our children.
- Being willing to help whenever we are asked to.

One key reminder is for grandparents and parents to recognise that they are also in partnership with God, who is at work in their families. God is always in the picture—indeed, He is the main Person in all our stories, relationships, and interactions. As Paul wrote, "We are fellow workers in God's service" (1 Corinthians 3:9; see also 2 Corinthians 6:1; 1 Thessalonians 3:2). It is God who is at work in us to align our will to His and to act accordingly (Philippians 2:13).

When Jesus is the Lord in the lives of both grandparents and parents, there will be harmony and effective partnership. And the grandchildren will be blessed.

Prayer

Holy and loving Father, I thank You that You, with Your Son and Your Spirit, are always at work in Your people's lives. Help me recognise that You are at work in my family. Help me set apart Jesus as Lord in my heart, and enable me to grow in Christlikeness. Help me be a positive influence on my children and grandchildren. Assist me in empowering my children as they parent their children, and in encouraging and supporting them by praying for them and lending a helping hand and listening ear.

Reflection

1. What is the difference between a relationship that is based on partnership, and one that is competitive? How can you ensure that your relationship with your grandchildren's parents is a positive partnership?

2. What are your struggles in relinquishing decision-making and control over your grandchildren's upbringing and wellbeing? How can you overcome these by God's grace and power?

3. How can you demonstrate to your grandchildren that you love their parents? Make a list of specific things you can do in the coming days, and act on them.

4. Reflect on your partnership with God as you exercise love and responsibility in your family. How can you pray for your children and their spouses in their parenting role and responsibility?

---

[1] Nancy Wilson, "Honor Your Grandchildren's Father and Mother", https://www.desiringgod.org/articles/honor-your-grandchildrens-father-and-mother.

19

Becoming Friends

From time to time, pastors come to me for counsel regarding problems they are facing, and guidance in decision-making. When I was serving as a bishop, they tended to come from other denominations or churches where I did not have any say or authority. After I retired and no longer held any official position, they came from all over, including the denomination that I served in. We can understand this: people may be hesitant to seek counsel from those who have direct authority over them. But they are happy to do so from someone outside the system, so to speak.

This principle applies to families, too. Children do share things with their parents and consult them, and rightly so. But they may not be willing to open up fully, as their parents have direct authority over them and may react negatively. On the other hand, they may have less apprehension about opening up to their grandparents. A child might tell his grandmother about being bullied in school more readily than he would tell his parents, or about his difficulty understanding his maths lessons.

Not all children are comfortable sharing their secret struggles and anxieties with the seniors in the family. That is why there is a growing need for resident counsellors in our schools. Nevertheless, there is potential for grandparents and their grandchildren to have a nourishing, nurturing, and friendly relationship. This, of course, takes time to develop.

It begins in the heart of the grandparent. There is a difference between owning one's children and holding them in trust as stewards. The former leads to a toxic relationship between parents and children, while the latter allows children to bloom into the persons God created them to be.

For instance, one mother prayed on the day her daughter was getting married: "Heavenly Father, I thank and praise You for blessing me with this lovely daughter 25 years ago. With Your help, I did my best to provide her with a happy home and raise her up in Your ways. Thank You for being with me and my husband as we brought up our children. Today, I return this daughter You gave me back to You. As she gets married, she is leaving my home. I will still care for her in an appropriate way. But she is leaving the nest, and I ask that You will be with her and her husband. Watch over them and lead them in Your path. Protect and provide for them."

This mother demonstrated that she was able to love her daughter as one entrusted with the sacred trust of parenting one of God's precious children. If she had held on to her daughter as her possession, she would have done and would continue to do damage. She would not really love her daughter, and whatever love she felt would have been, in reality, self-love. Many parents relate to their children out of self-love. They are the ones who drive their children to dysfunction because they are using their children to soothe the needs of their own ego. The apostle Paul tells us not to "embitter" or "exasperate" our children (Colossians 3:21; Ephesians 6:4).

The key difference between owning one's child (or grandchild) and holding them in trust is genuine godly love. Such love thinks not of the self but of the other. It does not mean that parents should spoil their children by being permissive, and not disciplining or restraining them when they behave badly or are learning bad habits. The Bible connects love with truth (Ephesians 4:15) and with discipline (Proverbs 13:24; Hebrews 12:6). In other words, it is the love for our children that leads us to discipline them. When a mother sends her little son to a room for a time-out, her heart will feel for him. But she resolves to administer the discipline for his long-term good. Love, and proper and appropriate discipline, go together.

What is true for parents is also true for grandparents. We are to have true love for our grandchildren, and not just see them as an extension of ourselves. We do not own them, but we hold them in trust.

If we see our grandchildren as little friends to love selflessly, rather than possessions that we control, manipulate, and experiment with, then we have a great opportunity to bless them. You can demonstrate your friendship with your grandchildren by:

- Being available for them. Be approachable and give them a listening ear.
- Finding ways of doing things with them. Go for walks in the park, or visit the library, museum, or playground.
- Being willing to have fun with them, to laugh, and to be transparent.
- Playing age-appropriate games with them.
- Building trust between you and them.
- Taking time to have one-on-one interactions with them. (In the 18th century, Susanna Wesley made it a point to set aside specific times each week for each of her 10 children. Among her children, God raised John and Charles to lead a historic revival.)
- Praying with them when they share difficulties.
- Not being quick to be judgmental.

- Being a friend who they know loves them and with whom they can share at any time.

Grandchildren have a way of awakening something in our hearts. As someone observed, "A grandchild fills a space in your heart that you never knew was empty." As parents, we are often too task-oriented and anxious about succeeding, or stressed out by multiple responsibilities. But as grandparents, we are more at ease, wiser, and have less need for achievements. We have a second chance of blessing our offspring. We can truly become friends to them.

Prayer

Heavenly and loving Father, I confess that I made many mistakes parenting my children. I was too busy, preoccupied, anxious, inexperienced, and impatient. Now, I am older, more mellow, wiser, and more at peace. Thank You for giving me a second chance to do it better, with the grandchildren You have blessed me with. Help me to genuinely love them for their own sake and to hold them in trust, recognising that they belong to You more than they belong to me or my children. Help me to become their friend and to be willing to lay down my life for them through sacrificial and caring love that will not smother them but will nourish them with Your love.

Reflection

1. Reflect on the difference between "owning" our children and grandchildren, and holding them in trust for the Lord who has given them to us. How would this be seen in our attitudes, conversations, and actions?

2. What are the signs of loving others with self-centred love, and those of loving them with self-giving love? How can you grow in self-giving love? Why is it necessary to keep our eyes fixed on Jesus to do this (Hebrews 12:2)? Why did Jesus instruct us to love one another "as I have loved you" (John 13:34)? How does our walk with Jesus affect the way we walk with our grandchildren?

3. Reflect on some of the suggestions on how we can nurture friendship with our grandchildren. Which of these appeal to you? Which of these could you try out soon? Are there other ideas that come to mind?

4. Prayerfully reflect on why and how Abraham became known as a "friend of God" (2 Chronicles

20:7; Isaiah 41:8; James 2:23). How can there be a friendship between the eternal God and a finite and flawed human being? What did God do to build that friendship? What lessons are there for grandparents?

20

***

Grandparenting through the Stages

How quickly our grandchildren grow! From time to time, my wife and I receive from our children old photos of our grandchildren—when they were helpless and speechless toddlers. We always marvel at how quickly they have grown into chatty and active children, with voracious reading habits and growing knowledge, and with skills to beat us in board games.

It reminds us of the musical, *Fiddler on the Roof*, about the story of a poor Jewish milkman and his family. At the wedding of one of his daughters, Tevye sings a poignant song about how quickly his children have grown up, and asks, "Wasn't it just yesterday when they were small?" If you take a look at the lyrics (which you can find online), you may find them most meaningful.

If you take the 18-year period in your life when your grandchildren come along (say, 50 to 68), the changes in them would be far more obvious than the changes in you. They would change physically (from tiny babies to fully-grown young adults), in their mental abilities (with increasing language abilities to the point that they can give you vocabulary and grammar lessons), social reach, and spiritual capacity. Jesus himself is described as a child who "grew in wisdom and stature, and in favour with God and man" (Luke 2:52).

As our grandchildren grow, how we relate with them will also need to take some significant turns. When we can no longer carry them like we could when they were tiny toddlers, how should we relate with them?

Deuteronomy 6:1–9 provides instruction on how we ought to relate with children at different stages of their lives. Moses reveals that God had commanded him to teach the Israelites (v. 1), who are then to teach their children and their children's children (v. 2). They are to teach their children the truth about God and to love Him wholeheartedly (vv. 4–5), and to do this using many methods: impressing, discussing, and reminding (vv. 6–9).

Notice the methods employed in teaching these truths. I deal with these in greater detail in another book, *Raising the Next Generation: Meditations on Parenting.*[1] Verses 8–9 say: "Tie them as symbols on your hands and bind them on your foreheads. Write them on the door-frames of your houses and on your gates." And before that, in verse 7, Moses says: "Impress them on your children. Talk about them when you sit at home and when you walk along the road, when you lie down and when you get up."

Here, you can see a sort of developmental theory on teaching different groups of children. When they are very young, children are impressionable and easily influenced. I remember one of my granddaughters saying that she would like to be a writer, like her *thatha* (grandfather). At this malleable age, we can teach children best by simply being good role models for them to imitate. They are always watching how we speak, what attitudes we display, and how we behave. These impressions shape their foundational values and become significant memories.

As children grow up, however, our methods of interacting with them need to evolve. It is no longer enough to simply model right behaviour. At kindergarten- and primary school-going age, our grandchildren become talking, questioning, and arguing little people. Their vocabulary grows by leaps and bounds. Then begins the period that is characterised by endless questions. Why does the sun set every day? Why should we keep quiet in church? Why can't I have chocolate now? Why do you wear glasses? And on and on it goes.

With such developing minds and inquisitiveness, we can use the second method proposed by Moses: talking with children when you sit at home or when you walk along the road. At this stage, it is good to explain or reason with them why certain behaviours are appropriate and others are not. We do this in the hope that they will not only do what is right, but also understand in their hearts why they need to do so.

Then, there will come a time when impressions and discussions are no longer effective. Teenagers do not like to be lectured; they do not like to be told what to do. Moreover, their contacts and relationships with peers, in person and online, will become more important to them. You will find that you are increasingly in the margins of their world, and will have to accept that and continue to be a blessing to your grandchildren.

At this stage, our instruction becomes less overt. It is more important to be a grandparent-friend who is available to them, someone they can run to when they are hurt, lost, or confused. When the opportunity presents itself, such as when they seek your advice, you can gently remind them of the good things they have learnt from their parents and you, and what they had discovered in Sunday school and church. As Moses says, "Tie them as symbols on your hands and bind them on your foreheads. Write them on the door-frames of your houses and on your gates" (vv. 8–9). If we have laid the groundwork when they were children, they should not need more than a simple reminder of their earlier lessons.

When our grandchildren become adults, we can still relate with them as friends and sounding boards, as encouragers and prayer partners.

All this tells us that we must adapt our relationship with our grandchildren to their stages of development. Research shows that most people (67 percent) received Christ into their lives before the age of 18.[2] A similar survey found that 63 percent made a commitment to Christ when they were between 4 and 14 years old, a period known as the 4–14 window. This is a period that is ripe for spiritual harvest, and we can prayerfully be available to God and our grandchildren to bring them patiently, wisely, and lovingly to Christ.

Prayer

Loving and righteous Father, I thank You for the grandchildren You have given to me and my spouse. Help us be a positive influence in their lives as You give us wisdom to relate to them in a way that brings out the best in them, the best that You have already planted. Help us be good role models as they watch us closely and help us find time to engage meaningfully in conversation with them as we fill our words with Your grace and love. May our words bring healing and guidance. Help us be available to our older grandchildren, reminding, encouraging, and walking alongside them. Fill us with Your love and wisdom.

Reflection

1. Reflect on Deuteronomy 6:1–9. What are the key lessons in the text? Compare the lessons with your experience of parenting. Are there things you would have done differently if given another chance? Consider how your grandchildren provide you with a new opportunity.

2. Reflect on what you would like to discuss with your grandchildren. Are they asking questions that you find difficulties talking about? Why? How can you be a good conversation partner, without appearing to be domineering or hypocritical? What are some questions or topics that you should be introducing to your grandchildren soon?

3. What are some difficulties you have with your teenage grandchildren? Or, if you are not there yet, what are your observations of the struggles your fellow grandparents are facing? What cultural and worldview differences can you find between your grandchildren and you? How do you think you can bridge the gap?

4. How can you positively remind and encourage your grandchildren to keep in the Christian way, following Christ and being part of His church?

---

[1] Robert M. Solomon, *Raising the Next Generation: Meditations on Parenting* (Grand Rapids: Discovery House, 2019), Section 2 ("Parenting According to God's Law").

[2] According to a study in 2004 by the Barna Group which conducted interviews of 992 born-again Christians in the US, https://www.barna.com/research/evangelism-is-most-effective-among-kids/. The study also showed more positive responses to outreach influences among young people than among older people. See also details of a survey by the National Association of Evangelicals in 2015, https://www.nae.net/when-americans-become-christians/. While the figures may vary in different contexts, the general reality applies widely.

21

Listening:

Developing Grandparent Ears

In his book *Directions*, James Hamilton shares this insight about listening:

Before refrigerators, people used icehouses to preserve their food. Icehouses had thick walls, no windows, and a tightly fitted door. In winter, when streams and lakes were frozen, large blocks of ice were cut, hauled to the icehouses, and covered with sawdust. Often the ice would last well into the summer.

One man lost a valuable watch while working in an icehouse. He searched diligently for it, carefully raking through the sawdust, but didn't find it. His fellow workers also looked, but their efforts, too, proved futile.

A small boy who heard about the fruitless search slipped into the icehouse during the noon hour and soon emerged with the watch.

Amazed, the men asked him how he found it.

"I closed the door," the boy replied, "lay down in the sawdust, and kept very still. Soon I heard the watch ticking."[1]

Listening is an essential aspect of having a meaningful conversation or experiencing a growing relationship. The Bible emphasises the importance of listening—to God and others. Jesus told a large crowd: "Whoever has ears to hear, let them hear." He also said: "Therefore consider carefully how you listen" (Luke 8:8, 18).

In the most practical epistle in the New Testament, James exhorts his fellow Christians to be "quick to listen" and "slow to speak" (James 1:19). If we speak but do not listen, we are giving a lecture. If we listen and speak, we are having a conversation.

How, then, can we listen better to our grandchildren (and children) when we are having conversations with them?

To be a good listener, we must overcome certain bad habits. During a conversation, many of us fail to pay attention to what the other person is saying because we are too busy formulating our responses to what they are saying, or cutting in to speak over them. We may also be too distracted or preoccupied with other things to really listen. When a grandchild comes to us to show his artwork, we might look at it momentarily and mutter something before going back to whatever we were doing. We might fail to understand that what the child is looking for is some commendation and a conversation on what he has drawn—who the figures in his drawing are, and what the other details mean. Other adults may have also seen the drawing but failed to appreciate it or engage with it, and the child may have come to us, the grandparent, precisely to receive those things.

Hearing is a physiological act, as the sound of a person's voice registers in our ears and minds. But it does not necessarily mean that we are taking in what the other person is saying. In contrast, "active listening" pays attention to the whole person who is speaking: to his or her words, experiences, thoughts, emotions, anxieties, aspirations, frustrations, and hopes. In active listening, we listen with an attitude of really seeking to understand the other person. This kind of listening helps us build good relationships.

To be someone with whom our grandchildren feel safe to share their thoughts, we need to be mindful of our body language when we interact with them. It is said that only 7 percent of our communication comes across through our words, 38 percent through our voice cues, and 55 percent through facial cues.[2] This explains why it is always better to have a conversation face to face. It is possible for people to lie on a phone or to fail to discern the emotional condition of the other person on the line. It also explains why when we talk to children, we should encourage eye contact. When we tower over little children as we speak to them, it is unlikely that we will have a true conversation. The child might feel intimidated or feel that the adult is distant.

We can learn from the way Jesus related to children. He paid attention to them and showed that He recognised their presence. He took them in His arms and blessed them (Mark 10:16). We have seen paintings of children seated on Jesus' lap as He spoke to them. We can imagine that the children who saw Him knew that He loved them and felt acknowledged by an adult.

When we speak to a child, it is always good to do it eye to eye. It helps to squat down to be at the same height as the child, or to raise him or her up to where we are, so that we can truly communicate with both our words and facial expressions. At the same time, we can also pay attention to what they are saying and how they are saying it. This will make us better at listening.

Educator and writer Parker J. Palmer highlights an important key in reaching out to the souls of others. He says: "If we want to support each other's inner lives, we must remember a simple truth: the human soul does not want to be fixed, it wants simply to be seen and heard. If we want to see and hear a person's soul, there is another truth we must remember: the soul is like a wild animal—tough, resilient, and yet shy. When we go crashing through the woods shouting for it to come out so we can help it, the soul will stay in hiding. But if we are willing to sit quietly and wait for a while, the soul may show itself."[3]

When our grandchildren come to us to speak, there are several things we can do so as to be intentional in engaging them. We can put away our mobile phones or turn off the television to spend that precious time with them. Many children look for a listening ear and an observant eye when they try to communicate with the seniors in the family. But when they are neglected one too many times, they will stop coming to them in the same way.

Let us therefore develop "grandparent ears"—ears seasoned by life, shaped by wisdom, and sharpened by love, ears that are ready to listen with care and compassion, ears that can be trusted and sought.

The Bible consistently describes God as one who turns His ears to His children. The psalmist writes:

"The eyes of the LORD are on the righteous, and his ears are attentive to their cry . . . The righteous cry out, and the LORD hears them; he delivers them from all their troubles" (Psalm 34:15, 17; see also 1 Peter 3:12).

We not only have a speaking God but also a listening God—what a comforting truth! Like Him, we should take time to turn our eyes and ears to our grandchildren, to listen to them, and to make a difference in their lives.

Prayer

*Holy and loving Father, You have assured us in Your
Word that Your eyes are on Your children, and Your
ears listen to what Your children long to tell You.
Indeed, You love us in such profound ways.
You have commanded us to listen to Your Son,
who taught us to listen carefully. Help us to listen
to You and to others. In our interactions with our
grandchildren, help us to listen actively so that they
know they have been heard and acknowledged.
Bless us with grandparent ears as we learn
from You and Your Son Jesus.*

Reflection

1. List some people who have been good listeners in your life. What do you think made them listen well? Do you remember anyone who listened well to you when you were a child? How did they help you?

2. Reflect on your relationship with God and how listening is an important part of it. What is active listening, and how can we learn to listen to the whole person?

3. How can you reduce your distractions and preoccupations so that you can pay good attention to your grandchildren?

4. What are some practical lessons you have learnt from this chapter? What can you do or change to have a better listening ear for your grandchildren?

---

[1] James D. Hamilton, *Directions: Insights for Christian Living* (Kansas City, MI: Beacon Hill, 1976), https://www.preaching.com/sermon-illustrations/illustration-listening/.

[2] Albert Mehrabian, *Silent Messages* (Belmont, CA: Wadsworth, 1971). Mehrabian's findings were nuanced and have been popularly misunderstood as an inflexible formula. The lesson is the importance of non-verbal cues.

[3] Parker J. Palmer, *The Courage to Teach: Exploring the Inner Landscape of a Teacher's Life* (San Francisco: John Wiley & Sons, 1997). Quoted in Plough Publishing, *Daily Dig: To See and Hear* (campaign-archive.com).

22

Praying for Your Grandchildren

Lillian Penner, the author of *Grandparenting with a Purpose*, writes about a letter she had found in her family archives. It was written by her great-grandfather in Poland to her grandfather, who had migrated to the United States. In it, she found this striking line: "I faithfully pray for you, for your children, and for your future generations." What a precious experience it is to discover one's prayerful great-grandfather![1]

Few things can compare with the joy, tenderness, and intensity of praying for our grandchildren. I know of grandparents whose grandchildren live overseas, and of missionary couples who are themselves overseas and away from their grandchildren in their home countries. Separated by distance, these grandparents miss interacting actively with their fast-growing grandchildren. Though there are now means to connect online, these joyful (and noisy) moments are short-lived. Yet, it does not mean that our connection with them ceases after we switch our screens off or when our grandchildren leave our homes. We can still remain connected to them by praying for them.

It is important that our connection with our grandchildren is undergirded by our connection with the living God. We have a great privilege of bringing our grandchildren to the Lord and into His light and grace. During Jesus' earthly ministry, people brought little children to Him (Matthew 19:13–15; Mark 10:13–16; Luke 18:15–17). Most of us assume, reasonably so, that it must have been the parents who did so, but the Gospels do not actually mention who brought them to the Lord. Could it be that some of them were grandparents? This is possible, especially as we remember that families then were multi-generational.

We, too, can and should bring our grandchildren to God. One of the key ways to do this is through prayer. As many parents today tend to be busy—loaded as they are with endless tasks, responsibilities, and worries—grandparents can faithfully pray for their grandchildren with wisdom and love. We can spend unhurried time talking to God about the little ones, asking for His protection and blessings on them.

What should we pray for our grandchildren? There are common petitions that grandparents generally pray: for their grandchildren's education, health, protection, and development. Luke 2:52 records that Jesus, as a child, "grew in wisdom and stature, and in favour with God and man". This verse refers to Jesus' physical, intellectual, social, and spiritual development. It provides us with a good starting point on how we can cover our grandchildren in prayer.

But instead of just skimming through some general petitions, we can also learn to take time to dwell more deeply in prayer.

For example, when praying for the *intellectual* development of our grandchildren, we can pray that they will get to appreciate the truths of God and internalise them, and that they will read the Bible and good literature that will shape them well.

Or, when we are praying for their *social* development, we can pray for their social contacts in school and on social media, and for protection against bad influences. We can use Psalm 1 to pray that our grandchildren will grow up to be like trees planted by streams of living water (v. 3).

And when we pray for our grandchildren's *spiritual* growth, we can specifically pray that they will come to faith in God, be able to relate to Christ, and be led by the Spirit in their daily lives. We can pray that they will develop an appetite for God's Word, and that they will learn to trust God and be obedient to Him.

One way we can pray specifically for our grandchildren is to use Scripture. God may put in our hearts certain truths and instructions as we read the Bible in the morning. We can then direct our hearts to pray those verses or Bible truths into the lives of those we are praying for, including our grandchildren.

For example, we might read Isaiah 5:20 about how things may be twisted and inverted in this sinful world, where evil is seen as good and good as evil, darkness is celebrated as light, and light denounced as darkness. In a world where values and moral behaviour become confusing, we need to pray that God will protect our grandchildren from the sinful patterns of this world. They need to be grounded well in the ways and wisdom of God.

Or, we might be reading the parable of the sower (Matthew 13:1–23), and thus pray that our grandchildren will flourish like the seed in the good soil as they are led by their parents and Sunday school teachers to think about God.

There are countless ways we can pray for our grandchildren, that they will:

- Fear God (Job 28:28)
- Be directed to make the right decisions and choices (Psalm 32:8; Isaiah 30:21)

- Have a teachable heart (Proverbs 2:1–2)
- Grow in Christlike character and humility
  (Colossians 3:12–13; 1 Peter 5:5)
- Develop love and compassion for others (James 2:8)
- Act responsibly and honestly (Psalm 34:13)
- Develop good social and spiritual habits (Matthew
  25:42–46)
- Have God's supernatural help when going through
  difficulties (Psalm 9:9; 46:1)

At times, we might find ourselves in situations where we are troubled by what we see in our grandchildren. It might be repeated bad behaviour, being influenced negatively by their friends, or getting into situations that may harm them. This may cause a deep burden in our hearts as we pray for troubled and wayward grandchildren. There might be times when we do not know what to pray for or how to pray. In such times, we have God's promise that He will help us in such situations:

> In the same way, the Spirit helps us in our weakness. We do not know what we ought

to pray for, but the Spirit himself intercedes for us through wordless groans. And he who searches our hearts knows the mind of the Spirit, because the Spirit intercedes for God's people in accordance with the will of God. (Romans 8:26–27)

The Spirit understands our groaning and groans with us in prayer. He knows the will of God and will enable us to pray. Our Lord Jesus is also praying for us and our loved ones (Romans 8:34). We are thus greatly strengthened when our family, including our grandchildren, are brought into the divine vortex of God's love. This happens when we pray.

A praying grandparent can be a great comfort to other family members. Families go into crisis mode from time to time. In such situations, a praying grandparent can be a calming presence, providing the wisdom, peace, and encouragement that comes from God. What a blessing we can be!

Prayer

Dear heavenly Father, I am greatly encouraged that Your Son and Your Spirit are interceding for Your children on earth. Help me join this heavenly intercession by praying for my children and grandchildren. Enable me to bring my burdens and hopes to You in prayer. Help me find unhurried time to spend time with You and to be able to tell You about each of my grandchildren. I know You care for them and that You want to bless them. Remind me to faithfully pray for my family and grandchildren. Give me this burden and fill me with Your love.

Reflection

1. Reflect on how you intercede for your family members regularly. Is it something that needs greater attention, regularity, and depth?

2. Make a list of specific things you can pray for each of your grandchildren. Do any Bible passages come to mind when you make such a list? Use the list to faithfully pray for your grandchildren.

3. Try applying passages you read in your quiet time when you pray for others. After doing this for a while, reflect on the difference this makes to your prayer life.

4. See if you can discern what Jesus and the Spirit may be praying for your grandchildren. If you discern anything, pray along with the Spirit and the Son.

---

[1] Lillian Penner, "Four Powerful Ways Praying Grandparent Make a Difference", https://www.crosswalk.com/faith/prayer/4-powerful-ways-praying-grandparents-make-a-difference.html. See Lillian Penner, *Grandparenting with a Purpose: Effective Ways to Pray for Your Grandchildren* (Enumclaw, WA: Redemption Press, 2015).

23

Grandparenting in the Church

There is a great need to understand the scope and depth of the Christian life. The apostle prayed that believers would be able "to grasp how wide and long and high and deep is the love of Christ" (Ephesians 3:18). God's love and care for His creation is far beyond our comprehension and limited grasp.

It is especially important to realise this at a time when we see rampant individualism in popular culture. This is the age of the "Me" generation that lives in self-centredness and self-indulgence. Even in the church, we come across a grossly limited view of the Christian life—one that is reduced dangerously to a "Me and my God" philosophy and lifestyle.

To counteract this extreme individualism, many pastors and church leaders are attempting to highlight the importance of family, and this is good. With the rising incidence of family dysfunction, this has become even more urgent. Marriage and parenting are deemed to be pressing issues. It is necessary for the church to emphasise the key role that healthy, godly families play in the church and in society.

However, individualism can create an insidious "my family and God" philosophy that reduces God's interest in us to just our own families. We want our loved ones to be saved, and we seek God's blessings for them. Beyond that, we do not have much concern about others and the larger world. Some theologians have highlighted this as a new idolatry—the idolatry of the family.[1]

We need to heed this warning. While keeping a healthy focus on the family, we must also enlarge our vision and concern to larger realities. The New

Testament dwells largely on the church as a family of diverse peoples and ages. God is our Father, and we are the household of faith (Galatians 6:10). Our relationships in the church are familial: older men are fathers, older women are mothers, and younger people are brothers and sisters (1 Timothy 5:1–2).

Beyond the church, we can think of the larger society of people who are in need, and beyond that, of all history where God is at work. God is reconciling the whole world to himself in Christ (2 Corinthians 5:19), and His concerns and purposes are as vast as His universe, the heavens, and the earth. To be His children and the disciples of Christ is to share the scope and depth of His love.

We can apply this truth to our roles as grandparents, and see that our ministry is not confined to the four walls of our homes; it is to flow out into the life and ministry of the church and beyond.

In the church, there are families of different kinds. Some families are struggling, without a father or mother, without grandparents, or are going through stress and dysfunction of different kinds. It is in this context that our grandparenting roles and responsibilities can take on new dimensions.

In the previous chapter, we looked at how we can and should pray for our grandchildren. We can also do this as a group of grandparents in church. We can get together as grandparents for fellowship, mutual encouragement, and prayer. We can share our prayer concerns with one another, such as when a grandchild is going through an illness or facing new challenges and transitions (like school postings and National Service). If there is enough trust in the group, more sensitive matters may be shared—for example, a grandchild who is having problems adjusting in school or dropping out of the faith. For this to happen, the motivation for gathering should not be nosiness but mutual care and concern. In this way, we need not confine our prayers to the welfare and spiritual growth of our own grandchildren; we can also include other children in the church.

We can also see if there are any members of our congregation who are in need of some help: single-parent families, parents struggling to bring up their children, children and teenagers who lack interactions

with grandparents (perhaps because the latter
have passed away, live far away, or are not actively
engaged) and would benefit if we went alongside and
encouraged them.

Grandparents are often kept on the sidelines
of ministries in the church. It is a pity because
grandparents and seniors can provide helpful inputs
and insights. For example, why are grandparents not
usually involved in Sunday school? Can they not be
Sunday school teachers or assistants? Their presence
can add value to the time spent by children in Sunday
school or other children's ministries. Their years of
wisdom can bring calm understanding and patient
encouragement to a troubled child. In the same way,
how many times do we see grandparents involved in
leading worship services and singing? Grandparents
in the worship team can bring in new dimensions
and perspectives to enrich the life and worship of the
congregation. If your church does not encourage or
has not seen the potential of involving grandparents in
some of its ministries, why not let them know of your
availability and that of your fellow grandparents?

From time to time, the church can bring together grandparents and their grandchildren in an activity that encourages interaction and sharing. This can be in the form of a half-day camp ("grandcamp"), a picnic, or an event where grandchildren can share their perspectives and questions, and grandparents can also tell their stories, relate their experiences, and share their faith.

The church can also organise special seminars for grandparents to help them think and pray through their grandparenting responsibilities and opportunities. They can discuss their struggles and difficulties, and learn about the sub-cultures in which their grandchildren are growing up and what they can do to provide Christian nurture and guidance. This will assure grandparents that they have the support of the church, and that they are not alone or forgotten.

The early church was inter-generational and has been so for very long, until nuclear families became the norm more recently. We tend to exacerbate the situation by separating the various generations in church into their own "silos", so to speak. The way we do church may segregate the generations and reduce (or even destroy) inter-generational interaction. This is not helpful, and the church must think about how it can be truly an inter-generational body, both in theory and practice.

In this effort to do church in a more effective framework, with long-term implications, grandparents do have a critical role to play. This is something that must be recognised by all.

Prayer

Heavenly Father, help me to connect with Your heart—a Father's heart—more and more, and to recognise the scope and depth of Your love. Enable me to realise that You love me and my family, and to be grateful to You. Help me to also recognise that Your heart extends to other families in the church. Give me the eyes of Your Son Jesus, who saw people as harassed, helpless, and like sheep without a shepherd. Help me to be compassionately involved in their lives and to be an instrument of Your loving hands. Help me to connect with other grandparents for mutual encouragement and prayer so that we can all fulfil Your eternal purposes for us and our families.

Reflection

1. Reflect on the larger purposes of God that include you, your family, your church, your society, and the world. Why is it important to bear this bigger picture in mind as a way of avoiding a narrow perspective of following Christ?

2. Consider how you can get together with other grandparents in your church to encourage one another and pray for your families. How can you make this a positive experience?

3. Reflect on the discussion above on how the local church and grandparents can work together to bless families and younger generations. Can you think of something specific that you can personally be involved in?

4. Make a list of people in your church who might be blessed if you went alongside them in some grandparenting ministry. Pray for them and seek to act accordingly.

5. Prayerfully reflect on the lessons and insights you have gained by reading this book. Discern what the Lord may be saying to you to encourage you and spur you to faithful action. List what these are, and spend time worshipping and thanking God for His blessings and presence.

---

[1] Janet Fishburn, *Confronting the Idolatry of Family: A New Vision of the Household of God* (Nashville: Abingdon Press, 1991).

About The Publisher

Discovery House Publishing™ produces a wide array of premium and quality resources that focus on Scripture, show reverence for God and His Word, demonstrate the relevance of vibrant faith, and equip and encourage you to draw closer to God in all seasons of your life.

Note To The Reader

We invite you to share your response to the message in this book by writing to us at:

5 Pereira Road, #07-01

Asiawide Industrial Building

Singapore 368025

or sending an email to:

dhpsingapore@dhp.org

www.ingramcontent.com/pod-product-compliance
Lightning Source LLC
Chambersburg PA
CBHW071738150726
47998CB00005B/1698